Steve Blease is a Mancunian. He spent over 30 years working in international insurance, with periods of residence in Europe, New Ze̶̶̶ ̶ ̶ ̶dle East. In 2006 he took a ga̶ ̶ ̶ ̶ ̶ ̶ ̶rom Land's End to John O'Groats. He is married with three grown up children and lives in Norwich.

END TO END

Steve Blease

Book Guild Publishing

Sussex, England

First published in Great Britain in 2008 by
The Book Guild Ltd
Pavilion View
19 New Road
Brighton, BN1 1UF

Typesetting in Times by
YHT Ltd, London

Printed in Great Britain by
Athenaeum Press Ltd, Gateshead

A catalogue record for this book is available from
The British Library.

ISBN 978 1 84624 201 4

For Jane

The End to End Route

1

It was on the way down from Bristol that I finally began to grasp the enormity of what I'd taken on. The train had left Bristol Temple Meads at around 1.15 that afternoon, and nearly four hours later we were still on the move. It seemed that every time I looked out of the window my mind would return, almost obsessively, to the fact that if I was going to do what I'd set out to do, I was going to have to walk back every single mile the train had covered. And if I managed that, I'd still only be about 20 per cent of the way towards my ultimate objective. It wasn't actually a bad feeling. Sure, there was a heavy element of self-doubt there – but my main feeling, as I sat comfortably in the middle of a troupe of chattering Japanese schoolchildren, was one of quiet exhilaration. I tried to savour it and fix it in my memory. It's not every day you contemplate a walk from Land's End to John O'Groats.

An unbroken journey from one end of Great Britain to the other is a major challenge, whatever the chosen mode of transport. It's a hell of a long way. But the distance from end to end is still within the compass of people's imagination, and, given a modicum of luck and stamina, getting there is not insuperable. The stretching but achievable nature of a Land's End to John O'Groats walk has made it an enduring target for generations of adventurers, fundraisers and athletes (not to mention the occasional lunatic). And it's not the exclusive preserve of walkers and cyclists. There's the guy with cerebral palsy who did it in his wheelchair and a man called Steve Fagan who took nine days to make the journey on roller skates. If his website was to be believed, someone called Petedangerous was working towards a Land's End to John O'Groats stilt walk in the spring of 2007.

And then there are the *real* eccentrics. The best known is surely Steve Gough, the Naked Rambler, whose end-to-end walk lasted from June 2003 to January 2004. Much of this time, of course, was spent in jail. Mr Gough's avowed rationale for making the journey was to question society's attitude towards the naked body. I lost count of the number of times I was asked whether I was going to provide a repeat performance.

Land's End to John O'Groats has a way of firing the imagination. It seems to represent something almost totemic in the British psyche, and a part of it had somehow rubbed off on me. I can't recall the precise moment it happened – I think it just gradually crept up on me – but at some stage in late 2005 I'd resolved to have a crack at it.

My motivation was not entirely clear – even, I must confess, to me. Sure, there were one or two sub-plots. For one thing, it would be good to see more of Britain. It had, for instance, been over 40 years since I'd made my one and only trip to Cornwall, and almost as long since I'd been to the Lake District. I'd never ventured north of Inverness. And I'd no idea what a Cotswold looked like. The trip would also (although I didn't want to place too much stress on this, at least publicly) fulfil a long-standing personal ambition to taste as many different local beers as possible.

But if I'm brutally honest I'd have to admit that there was a more substantial motivating force at work. This, I'm ashamed to say, was nothing more than a compulsive urge to show off. I'm not a walker – never have been – but as we've got older, and disencumbered ourselves of mutinous teenage children, my wife and I have bought ourselves some walking boots and done the occasional country walk. No doubt we'll do more in future as a way of keeping fit. We have friends and acquaintances who are into walking in a big way. Wouldn't it be great, when the conversation turned to walking, to be able to give a quiet, laconic response, Clint Eastwood style, with a steely glint in the eye, that, actually, I'd done 'End-to-End'? I'd have to work on the steely glint a little but I was sure that it would improve with a little practice.

But the final, clinching factor was the beguiling prospect of simply taking off. Putting a few things in a rucksack and just disappearing. No worries, no responsibilities. After more than 30 years behind a desk it was very enticing. I was lucky too, because my working life had reached a point where I could afford the time to do this crazy thing.

And now I'd actually committed myself by going and telling everyone what I was going to do. I had a choice. I could stay on the train and (gulp) push off from Land's End tomorrow morning. Alternatively, I could quietly rent a cottage in Cornwall, go 'underground' and return home claiming triumphant success in a couple of months or so. As the train was extending the scale of my task with every passing minute, the latter option began to look increasingly attractive.

But for the moment at least there were more immediate things to think about. The priority now was to fight my way clear of the Japanese schoolchildren, get me and the rucksack off the train at Penzance and then find Dave Dobson.

I'm not sure that visiting two pubs constitutes a 'crawl', but they were the only two pubs in Land's End, and Dave and I visited them both in rapid succession. Dave and I played cricket together for several decades before we both had to concede defeat to Father Time and retire from the game, thereby sparing our bodies further punishment and our souls further embarrassment. Dave was holidaying in

3

Cornwall and had offered to transport me the ten or so miles from the railway station at Penzance to the Land's End Hotel. Before I checked in we went to the Success Inn at Sennen Cove, where we introduced ourselves to Sharp's Doom Bar, before moving on to the First and Last Pub in England to sample the Cornish Blond beer. I decided that it sounded quite impressive to have started an end-to-end walk with a pub crawl at Land's End, so a 'crawl' is how it will go down in the annals.

After Dave had left I checked in at the Land's End Hotel and was immediately seized by another moment of self-doubt similar to those I'd experienced on the train. The moment was triggered by my complete inability to navigate the short distance from the reception desk to my allotted room. Even allowing for the Cornish beer and the eccentric geography of the hotel, this failure can only be ascribed to total, rank incompetence. Whatever the cause, I just couldn't find the room and had to return to reception to seek further directions. An embarrassing moment – especially as I'd just confided to the woman at the desk that I was hoping to walk to John O'Groats. If I couldn't find room 32, she must have dismissed as fantasy my intention of navigating a route to Northern Scotland.

The Land's End Hotel is an excellent base camp for a Land's End–John O'Groats walk. It's not luxurious but it's comfortable – and the food is good. I figured that I deserved a solid dose of comfort given the inevitably variable standards of accommodation I'd be facing in the days and (hopefully) weeks to come. I'd wondered if there'd be other guests at the hotel starting an end-to-end trip – either on foot or by bike. If there was any day with the prospect of a mass start from Land's End then today, 19 April, was it. Early spring is the perfect time to start northwards and this was immediately after the Easter holiday. At breakfast I'd almost expected a room full of identikit gung-ho young athletes boisterously discussing the intricacies of the route and exchanging views, larded with complex, technical jargon, about the merits and demerits of their cycles or walking equipment. I discovered I was quite relieved to find that there weren't any. Only one other table was occupied – and that by a married couple who didn't look at all boisterous or gung-ho.

So the foyer of the hotel was empty and eerily quiet as I hauled my rucksack downstairs and checked out. The only person to witness my departure was Sarah, the receptionist, who gave me a splendidly warm and effusive send-off. I suspected that word of my failure to navigate the route to my room had got around, that her encouraging valedictory words derived from a belief, perfectly justifiable in the circumstances, that I hadn't got a hope in hell of finding my way to John O'Groats and that my mission was doomed to an early and ignominious conclusion. But if she had doubts she kept them to herself and very kindly helped me with the registration process which is the compulsory precursor to any end-to-end journey.

It would be difficult to imagine a more prosaic and downbeat start to a Land's End–John O'Groats walk. The big moment had arrived – departure day – but the rest of the world just didn't want to know. For one thing the weather was the epitome of anti-climax. Just grey, dull and drizzly. And for another, there was nobody present to recognize or celebrate the event. There's not even any concrete evidence that it actually took place. I'm sure you've seen photographs of smiling, excited people, often attended by troupes of hangers-on and well-wishers, clustered around the fabled signpost at Land's End that indicates the distance to John O'Groats, New York and any other random destination of the individual's choosing. The pictures hint of the anticipation and excitement that attends the start of an expedition – or alternatively the relief and satisfaction generated at its end.

5

What I hadn't realized, naively, was that the signpost is a strictly commercial undertaking. Furthermore, the bloke who takes the pictures, and who supplies the letters that appear on the fingers of the signpost, doesn't begin his working day until the leisurely hour of 10 a.m. His scheduled arrival was more than an hour distant as I heaved my rucksack to the door of the hotel and I was far too impatient and keyed-up to wait around.

I wandered over to the white line in the road that marks the official start of all end-to-end journeys from Land's End. Obligingly, the word 'START' was painted on the tarmac in big, easy to follow letters. I wondered if I could ask some hapless bystander to take my photograph there. But the place was completely deserted and the heavy drizzle militated against any immediate prospect of passers-by either (a) materializing or (b) willingly getting wet while they fiddled around with my camera. I decided that posterity would have to take my departure from Land's End on trust.

I returned to the hotel and, outside the front door, found an empty space of around 200 square feet in which to haul the rucksack up on to my shoulders. I'd discovered that this process could trigger bouts of lurching and staggering pronounced enough to seriously endanger third parties or their property, unless they were safely situated outside a comfortably large exclusion zone.

Actually, the rucksack wasn't *that* heavy. It weighed around 25 pounds which, once I'd finished lurching and staggering, was quite manageable. After all, British infantry at the Battle of the Somme went over the top carrying packs weighing 60 pounds or more. I'd worked hard to keep the weight down and had rigorously eliminated all but the bare essentials.

The first major determinant of rucksack weight had been my proposed style of travel. Would I be camping and cooking my own food? If so, then I'd be carrying significant

6

additional weight in the shape of a tent, a sleeping bag, a stove and some cooking pots. Out of interest I scoured the Internet in an effort to research the approach adopted by other end-to-enders. I found a splendidly clear and helpful website composed by a guy called Mark Moxon, who'd originally opted for the self-sufficient approach. He listed the equipment he took on his walk and it was impressively, even intimidatingly, long. Mark had his tent and cooking gear but his list also included such disparate items as a sleeping-mat repair kit and water purification tablets. I was impressed – until I read that at some stage during his walk Mark had suffered tendon damage in his foot and had decided to parcel up all the camping gear and send it home. Another successful end-to-ender, a lady by the name of Christine Roche, had also adopted the camping strategy. Her planning and preparation had been remarkably thorough – she'd even sent food parcels on ahead to selected points along her route. This sounded quite glamorous and exciting. The establishment of secret food caches called to mind the SAS or an underground guerilla army.

But fundamentally this was an easy question to resolve. The walk was going to be arduous enough without the additional self-imposed rigours inherent in camping. Imagine ... you've just walked 15 miles, it's pouring with rain and you've now got to erect a tent in some farmer's miserable field. Having done *that* you've then got to set to and cook your meal over a small guttering flame. The nearest pub is miles away and you hope you've got a decent book to read by torchlight in your sleeping bag because that's the only available entertainment this evening ... No way. Hang the expense but I was opting for B&B accommodation.

So, no tent and no cooking gear. No sleeping bag – or even a sleeping-mat repair kit.

With the help of the lovely Lisa at our local Rohan shop I'd also been able to keep clothes to a minimum. In the words of Rohan's own promotional material, 'when laundry facilities are few and far between, travelling can become a rather aromatic experience'. The solution is the use of silver thread in garment manufacture. Apparently, the knowledge that silver is an odour inhibitor has been around since the days of the Wild West, and Rohan have adopted the technology to good effect. So, only two shirts and two pairs of trousers. And, yes, OK, to answer the obvious question, I was going to try to walk to John O'Groats on only two pairs of underpants.

A source of some surprise and mild irritation was the weight of the various gadgets I was taking. Although, to be exact, not the gadgets themselves – modern, whizzy gadgetry like mobile phones, small digital cameras and hand-held computers are, both individually and collectively, virtually weightless. It's the apparatus required to recharge the batteries of all this high-tech gear that is surprisingly clunky and burdensome.

I'd also reluctantly deferred to the superior wisdom of the huge body of punditry that surrounds the end-to-end walk and had added various safety features to the luggage. These included a whistle, a torch, a reflective yellow jacket and a tin-foil sleeping bag. In addition I'd packed enough maps to see me as far as Bath (well, you have to be optimistic) and sufficient protective clothing to withstand – hopefully – every potential vagary of the English and (if I was feeling *really* optimistic) Scottish climates.

All this in a 60-litre rucksack. No, I didn't know the capacity of rucksacks was measured in litres either. It would be interesting to conduct a test with a couple of crates of Stella.

The one piece of equipment that I'd really taken to, and already developed an affection for, was my pedometer. The information it gave was pretty standard. Time, number of steps, distance covered, calories expended. What was novel and exciting, however, was the way in which the information was conveyed. Of course, there was the normal digital display, but this was augmented by a most engaging and innovative audio feature. At the touch of a button the information available visually on the display screen was replicated by the voice of a Chinese lady, who announced the relevant statistic in a tone of gentle and helpful encouragement. She sounded extremely attractive, and the way she stumbled, in classic oriental fashion, over the 'r' and 'l' sounds in the word 'calories' was actually rather sexy.

And, like most Chinese ladies, she didn't weigh much either.

So this was it. I was travelling light and I was ready to go. No more preparation and planning. No more endless debates about routes and equipment. No more complacent basking in the admiration of friends, work colleagues and relatives. All the talk and speculation was over. It was time to perform.

If you study the literature of travel you'll notice that the description of a voyage or journey is often asymmetrical. The act of departure and the first few steps along the way are depicted in minute and loving detail, but as the journey progresses, and the novelty of the project begins to wear off, the description becomes increasingly foreshortened, and each successive component is treated with increasing brevity. There's a very good reason for this – namely the profound intensity of feeling and sheer excitement that attends departure and the first, faltering steps of the journey. It was just like that for me as I deliberately and rather self-consciously walked away from the Land's End Hotel. There *was* an intensity of feeling – a rare and turbulent mixture of emotions. Anticipation? Yes. Exhilaration? Definitely. Maybe a small element of apprehension too. Above all, a splendid feeling of freedom, of pushing off into the unknown. After a few seconds the mixture became a little too rich to handle. I started to laugh. The whole thing seemed unreal.

What the hell was I doing here? The very idea of this ageing, overweight insurance man with a dodgy back walking 1,100 miles to John O'Groats suddenly seemed so utterly and completely preposterous that laughter was the only rational response.

I was laughing so hard that I got lost. Yes, at Land's End. An implausible feat I grant you, but I managed it. It took me all of 15 seconds. I was aiming for the South West Coast Path which winds north-eastwards away from Land's End along the cliffs to Sennen Cove. Instead I crossed the START line, walked a short distance up the road and arrived at the exit to the mini theme park which is, in essence, Land's End. Sensing that I'd already somehow strayed off-piste, I asked directions from an official who was huddled in a kind of sentry box, sheltering from the drizzle. He turned out to be Australian and he pointed me in the direction of Sennen Cove. So, given also the previous night's fiasco in the hotel, I'd achieved the distinction of getting lost twice before leaving Land's End. And it had needed an Australian to put me right. The portents for the rest of the walk were not good.

The heady intensity of feeling stayed with me for a while as I walked along the cliffs. My mood was buoyed even further by a text from Jeff, a friend and fellow resident of my home village in Norfolk, who, with his wife Rosemary, had already done an end-to-end walk, albeit in chunks over a number of years. He and Rosemary now planned to repeat the journey, this time cycling, and they were already preparing for a departure early in May. Jeff wished me good luck.

'Step by step, mile by mile,' he said.

It didn't take me long to reach Sennen Cove. And the practicalities of the walk were now gradually starting to overlay the earlier feelings of excitement and exhilaration. It had stopped raining and was getting warmer. I was over-dressed and had to remove a layer of clothing. There was food to be bought at the shop in Sennen and I also had to work out where I was going to leave the Coast Path and head inland towards Penzance.

I cut away from the coast at the end of Whitesand Bay and headed due east uphill towards Chapel Carn Brae. The elevation and the improving weather gave me the first view of the walk – south over the 'toe' of Cornwall to the coast and the Atlantic beyond. I inspected Carn Euny, an Iron Age village with a 20-metre-long 'fogou' or covered chamber. And then promptly got lost again.

For some obscure reason I'd opted to kick off the walk with a detailed 1: 25 000 Ordnance Survey map rather than the less intricate 1: 50 000 versions I'd be using for the rest of the route. I got completely confused by the plethora of detail, failed to distinguish between the lines that denoted field edges and those that denoted paths and soon realised that I was off course for the third time in 24 hours.

Fortunately, it didn't take long to resume normal service, and the distinction of being the first lunch venue of the walk fell to the beautiful churchyard in the village of Sancreed, some five miles to the west of Penzance. I duly covered these miles in the course of a pleasant afternoon's walk in the spring sunshine along the quiet Cornish country lanes. It had been a relatively gentle, easy start but I'd broken my duck. I had ten miles under my belt. Only another 1,090 to go.

2

I was pleased with Day Two on the whole. Although the weather was poor and the going hard, I got into a rhythm and finished the day in good shape. The Cornish coastal scenery was bound to impress a resident of the Norfolk flatlands. And I also forged a new and highly entertaining friendship.

I'd felt a mild sense of achievement the previous evening. I'd explored Penzance and renewed my acquaintance with Sharp's Doom Bar, but in reality Day One had been little more than a gentle loosener. Ten miles in around five and a half hours was hardly dramatic progress. However, the leg from Penzance to Helston on 20 April presented a sterner challenge. Seventeen miles – mainly along the rough and undulating South West Coast Path – with a lousy weather forecast. This was no longer a rehearsal, this was the real thing.

I conscientiously breathed a few words into my Dictaphone before starting the day, and on listening to the words again several weeks later, it was clear that the previous day's feeling of unreality had entirely disappeared. The leaden skies, the drizzle and the slight stiffness in the limbs were all too real, and the tenor of the words was markedly less enthusiastic than that of the rather vapid recording I'd made in Land's End some 24 hours previously. There was a subfusc, but nonetheless pervasive, air of doubt and pessimism.

The mood was lightened by a long conversation with Richard, my host. While he ducked in and out, serving a comprehensive and gratifyingly cholesterol-rich English breakfast, we talked of the walk and of the challenges to come. Richard questioned the sanity of the whole undertaking. 'A man of your age ... ' But underneath the banter I had a distinct feeling that, for two pins, Richard would have abandoned his B&B that morning, shoved a few things into a rucksack and joined me on the road to John O'Groats. The conversation left me with a renewed sense of good fortune – how exceptionally lucky I was just to be able to walk off into the blue (or grey) yonder. Richard's day was well mapped out in advance and probably quite mundane. My own was much less predictable. I had very little conception of what the next few hours might hold in store. Richard wished me well and I hit the road at around 8.30.

The morning's walking was dry and relatively easy. The South West Coast Path out of Penzance follows the flat shoreline of Mounts Bay, dominated by St Michael's Mount and its medieval castle. Idyllic coastal scenery – with the added dimension of the railway that runs alongside the path and the helicopter traffic buzzing overhead to and from the Scilly Isles. Coffee in Marazion and then the undulating cliff path through Perranuthnoe and Prussia Cove to Sydney Cove.

The only event of note was the first of what proved to be a series of similar incidents that occurred with embarrassing regularity throughout the entire walk. My solitary existence was already inducing a tendency to exclaim out loud or mutter to myself – a tendency that was exacerbated in moments of frustration or impatience. Getting close to Cudden Point I had just launched upon a harmless round of cursing – the colourful nature of which was provoked by the pathetic inability of my large and inelegant fingers to operate my small and very elegant digital camera. Harmless the

13

cursing might have been, but it was also rather loud and emphatic – and obviously entirely audible to the man who appeared out of nowhere, walking the path on the other side of the hedge some two feet from where I was standing. Fortunately he disappeared just as quickly. All rather embarrassing really, although at least I hadn't been doing my Leslie Phillips impression.

By the time I got to Sydney Cove it had started to drizzle. The place presented a tableau of the archetypally depressing English seaside day. Grey sky, grey sea. A café with all its outdoor tables unoccupied and its selection of buckets, spades and plastic inflatables flapping forlornly in the wind. A poor woman on the beach working desperately hard to keep two kids in plastic macs amused – all huddled around a small sandcastle. They were the sole occupants of Praa Sands, which the guidebook described as a 'long golden sweep'. Not today, not today.

I had lunch and pressed on in the rain in the direction of Rinsey Head. The abandoned tin mines on the high cliffs were spectacular – probably the scenic highlight of the day – but they were not flattered by the sea fret and general gloom. I *was* impressed, however, by the building on Rinsey Head itself, which from afar looked like a ruined castle, but which on closer inspection proved to be a relatively modern house. It was totally isolated, grey, bleak and forbidding – something out of a Hammer House of Horror movie.

It was at this point, mid-afternoon on the cliffs in the rain, that I was suddenly overhauled by two walkers who, although fully laden, were making much quicker progress than me. Obviously a husband and wife team. Not young – I guessed at early/mid-sixties – but the immediate impression was one of leanness and vitality. This impression was reinforced in the course of our initial exchanges by the news that they too were headed for John O'Groats. The man, Roy, had a strong accent that I recognized. But any need for guesswork as to his origins was being rapidly eroded by the effervescent directness and amiable inquisitiveness that are the hallmarks of the true Mancunian. It seemed to take us about four seconds to establish that Roy, his wife Maureen and I shared not only a common destination but common origins as well.

We established that Roy and Maureen had arrived in Land's End the previous morning just in time to catch a glimpse of my disappearing back as I (eventually) found the path to Sennen Cove. They had signed the book at the hotel, and then in keeping with an approach to walking that was far more rigorous than my own, they had taken the much longer (16 miles) roller-coaster cliff path to Penzance, rather than the cosy 10-mile inland route favoured by dilettantes like myself.

Another six seconds and the conversation had turned to the inevitable Mancunian subject of football, but before Roy and Maureen forged ahead on the path to Porthleven we were also able to establish that Maureen and I were walking for a common cause in the shape of the NSPCC. In all the rain and general excitement we forgot to exchange phone numbers, so I fervently hoped that our paths would cross again. I had taken an immediate liking to Roy and Maureen, but I think, on reflection, that the main reason I was keen to keep track of them was their confidence, the very clear and immediate message that they were going to do this thing. Getting to John O'Groats was already a given; all that remained to be decided were a few minor route issues and what presents to take back for the grandchildren. I felt my own confidence increase a notch. If these guys were going to do it then so was I.

At Porthleven I turned inland for the last two remaining miles along the lanes into Helston. Depending upon the route I finally chose, my next encounter with the sea would be at Morecambe Bay or in the far north of Scotland.

Ambling out of Helston the next morning I reflected on

15

Day Two with some satisfaction. I'd managed a good steady day's walk in conditions that, while far from difficult, weren't perfect either. I'd had a distinct lift from meeting Roy and Maureen – not to mention Joyce, my landlady of the previous evening, who, besides being hospitality personified, had also, in her mid-seventies, gone to Peru and walked the Inca Trail.

Best of all, though, the weather had cleared and it was a splendid, fresh spring morning. I felt good.

In a previous life Joyce had managed the Texaco petrol station at the eastern edge of Helston. I stopped there to buy a cup of coffee and walked on north-eastwards. I'd always been mildly irritated by the sight of people stumbling around the City or Canary Wharf clutching a cardboard mug, but in these narrow Cornish country lanes it somehow, bizarrely, felt quite appropriate. The coffee, equally bizarrely, was strong and sustaining and lasted a good mile along the road to Boderwennack.

Much of the route for the next few days would be along country lanes. I'd traced out what I thought would be the best way to Truro, bearing in mind an obvious desire to avoid the busier roads. As a basic rule of thumb I'd assumed that the narrower and/or less brightly coloured a road appeared on the map the less traffic it would carry. This seemed to be working well as a basic precept until I passed the village of Carnkie. Here, for reasons that were difficult to fathom, an innocuous looking road that appeared thread-like on the map was transformed into something resembling the M6. The volume of traffic was immense. I was initially concerned and then terrified. Who were these people? Where were they going? What were they going to do when they got there? I'd already noticed that Cornish drivers didn't have much truck for pedestrians, and this straight, narrow road, with traffic moving along at about 100 mph, gave them every opportunity to practice the time-honoured Cornish sport of missing-the-pedestrian-by-the-narrowest-possible-margin. There had already been several occasions when I'd escaped death by a whisker, but when I saw this particular car, apparently completely out of control, barrelling straight towards me, I genuinely believed my moment had come. The only thought going through my head was how wise I'd been to undertake a root-and-branch review of my will before my departure. I clutched the hedge and waited for the end. The car screeched to a halt in a cloud of dust and rubber smoke about six inches away. The passenger window glided down and the driver, a charming middle-aged lady, utterly tranquil and serene, leant casually across. 'Terribly sorry to trouble you but do you happen to know the way to Carnkie?'

I was quite keen to ensure that I stayed in contact with Roy and Maureen. The weather hadn't leant itself to a lengthy conversation on the cliffs and I stupidly hadn't asked for a mobile number. I had the idea of calling the Land's End Hotel. Maybe when Roy and Maureen registered for the great end-to-end epic they'd left contact details. I stopped in Stithians to make some phone calls. Stithians, like Carnkie, did not appear to be a place where large volumes of money got spent. It was in Stithians that I saw a van carrying the legend 'Rag and Bone' – the first overt reference to this field of human endeavour I'd seen since *Steptoe and Son* in the 1960s.

The Stithians village seat was in a peculiar position, on a kind of raised pedestal virtually astride the wall of a small garden. This garden must have won the prize for best of class in the 'requiring minimal management' category. However, the annual management effort that the garden required – i.e. a cursory examination of the solitary pampas grass concoction – was obviously timed to coincide with my visit, because the pampas lady emerged about ten seconds after my arrival at the village seat, affording herself perfect audio-visual coverage of my phone calls. I drew a blank on the Roy and

Maureen front, wished the pampas lady good morning and carried on.

The highlight of the morning turned out to be a wonderful piece of serendipity. I'd taken my map to The Angel the previous evening, and over a pint of Doom Bar I'd traced my route along the lanes north-eastwards out of Helston until my index finger hit the hamlet of Cusgarne, beyond Stithians and about six miles south-west of Truro. The name brought me up with a jolt. Cusgarne, I recalled, had been the childhood home of a former girlfriend, and I made a stab at working out the maths. If my recollection was right I hadn't seen this particular lady in 34 years.

In the ordinary course of events I probably wouldn't have found the courage, but in the context of the bizarre and crazy venture on which I'd just embarked it somehow seemed the right thing to do. And in any case it was surely most unlikely that after all this time the family would still be *in situ*. Cusgarne is a tiny place and with the help of a passing postman I soon found the house. My knock was answered by a lady of considerably advanced years who, amazingly, confessed immediately to being my former girlfriend's mother. My first instinct was to panic, turn tail and rush off down the street. But the woman was behaving as if the arrival of a perspiring middle-aged vagrant, claiming to be a Land's End–John O'Groats walker, happened routinely every Friday morning. She brushed aside my stammered apologies and mumblings about intrusion, and invited me inside.

And despite her age this lady was as sharp as a tack. She recalled immediately that her daughter had once, in the mists of time, been wooed by a dissolute Mancunian student, and for the next 45 minutes or so we nattered companionably while she filled me in on what had befallen her daughter over the intervening 34 years. I was delighted to hear that life had been kind to her. That, and her mother's hospitality, made for a hugely enjoyable encounter.

I had lunch at Bissoe Arsenic Works. Now, not many people can say that.

Although there isn't a great deal left to see, Bissoe is a small piece of Cornwall's wonderful industrial heritage. You may not be aware (I certainly wasn't) that during the early nineteenth century Cornwall pioneered world arsenic production as a by-product of tin and copper mining. Most Cornish tin and copper mines had 'calciners', or burning houses, to separate out the arsenic and sulphur from the original ores. It was not until the nineteenth century that demand for arsenic arose, Bissoe's initial principal market being the Lancashire cotton industry which used it in pigments and dyes. Its use later spread to other industries – notably pharmaceuticals and pesticides. Bissoe was opened in 1834 and production continued until the onset of World War Two. There are uncorroborated reports that the Germans bombed the works during the war – Hitler didn't know it had closed.

There was one other event of note during my short sojourn at Bissoe – and one that I'd been anxious to avoid since Land's End. I fell over.

Right from the start I'd been uncomfortably conscious of the fact that it only needed a split second's inattention or one piece of fleeting bad luck to bring the whole project crashing down around my ears. 'Blease? Oh yeah, he was the guy who said he was going to walk to John O'Groats. Only got as far as Cornwall and then gave up. Twisted ankle or something. Wimp.' At the exit to the Arsenic Works I swung round in mid-stride to look at a signpost, got my feet in a tangle and came crashing down like a felled oak. It seemed to happen in slow motion; once I'd started to topple it felt like I had loads of time to correct the situation. The critical factor, however, was the rucksack. An additional 25 pounds weight attached to the upper body imparts significant and unaccustomed top-heaviness. This, allied to my inbred lack of coordination, easily offset my efforts to rectify the position. I hit the tarmac hard.

My knee was badly lacerated but my first concern was whether anyone had witnessed this fiasco. Fortunately, I seemed to have the Arsenic Works to myself, and the second, and most significant blessing was that my walking gear appeared to have escaped unscathed. The last thing I wanted was to have to walk to John O'Groats with my backside hanging out of my trousers.

After all this drama a gentle afternoon stroll into Truro. I used National Cycle Route 3, part of the burgeoning 'Sustrans' network of cycle paths. These are a boon to the long-distance walker which I soon came to admire greatly.

On arrival in Truro I went through the nightly ritual of the foot audit. I'll spare the reader the detail of this activity, but it basically consisted of a myopic and stiff-backed attempt to discover as much as possible about the way my feet looked and felt. Tonight they seemed OK.

So that was 44 miles covered since Land's End. My feet (and, on reflection, the rest of my body parts) were fine, it was a gloriously sunny evening and I was in a superb B&B in the Cathedral Close. My gracious hostess, Mary, had provided an excellent cup of tea on my arrival and I'd also had a bath. It felt absolutely wonderful.

And, if anything, even better after two pints of Kiddlywink – from Skinners, a Truro brewery. As it was such a fine evening the city was very busy but I found a spare table in The Old Ale House on Queen Street and enjoyed a seafood paella. And the final drop of satisfaction to be squeezed from the day was colliding with Roy and Maureen on my way back to the cathedral. We exchanged useful information about accommodation further up the trail, and this time we also exchanged phone numbers. This was not quite as straight-forward as it sounds. Roy seemed to eschew the use of technology altogether, and whilst Maureen did at least possess a mobile, her usage in the three years of ownership had been insufficient to trigger the need for the first top-up. It took her a while to come up with the number but she got there in the end. She made me, a complete Luddite in the eyes of my kids, feel like a real techno-buff.

And the next day, Saturday 22 April, was only a few hours old when I collided with my fellow end-to-enders again – this time at the entrance to Idless Wood as I walked north out of Truro. It was a glorious morning. I'd had a look around the cathedral before leaving the city along a quiet lane that ran alongside the River Allen. The scenery was rhapsodic. Roy and Maureen overhauled me and we walked together for an hour or so before our routes diverged. We were aiming for different destinations that night before coinciding again the following day. My estimation of Roy, already high, was even further enhanced when he revealed that he had been present to see Manchester United's Busby Babes play Real Madrid in their epic European Cup campaign of 1957. Not half bad for a Man City supporter, poor bloke.

I walked on through St Erme arriving around lunchtime at the picturesque village of Ladock. And here was another emerging recurrent theme of the journey. I happened upon the pub in Ladock, a very attractive place called The Falmouth Arms. The local brew, St Austell Ale, sounded promising and the pub looked exceptionally inviting in the spring sunshine. In fact 'inviting' was an understatement. The place exerted a kind of physical field force, a gravitational pull that drew me bodily towards the front door. Surely one pint wouldn't hurt. And wasn't I supposed to be engaged on some kind of 'research' into real ales of the United Kingdom, however ill-defined a piece of work this might be? The trouble was I knew that one pint would disappear as though by some massive and instantaneous process of evaporation. A second pint would be a necessity and, what with the need to eat lunch there, who knew where it might end? I was finding that age

21

was rapidly eroding my powers of recovery following even the lightest and most casual lunchtime imbibing; and I had a good few miles left to cover that day. I struggled against the field force, walked on and went to look at the church instead.

I was headed in the general direction of Indian Queens, but the general paucity of accommodation in the area had necessitated a slight eastwards kink in the route, which was now taking me towards Roche, some four miles distant. I was curious as to how Indian Queens acquired its name. One, exotic, explanation was that the 'Indian Queen' in question may possibly have been Pocahontas. But an inscription that once appeared above the porch of the former Indian Queen public house referred to a Portuguese princess who landed at Falmouth on a packet ship and stayed in the locality on her way to London. It is assumed that her dark olive skin caused her to be mistaken for an Indian. I wonder.

In any event the area is now much better known as the home of the Cornish Alps. These are the huge mounds of waste clay and quartz sand that are the by-products of Cornwall's china clay industry. And from the road out of Ladock the 'snow'-capped hills away to the north did indeed have a distinctly Alpine appearance. Closer to, the landscape looked a lot less wholesome. My route took me through Trethosa and Treviscoe, where the 'hills' and the massive concomitant holes in the ground looked exactly what they were – the ultimate in scarred industrial landscapes. It resembled the setting for a movie about one of those blighted places in rustbelt America, where all the inhabitants suffer from appalling pollution-related disease – before a feisty small-town lawyer (probably played by Julia Roberts) stands up and fights the greedy and cynical corporation that's been responsible for it all.

Day Four's walk from Truro to Roche had been a further 17 miles, although I discovered to my dismay that I couldn't measure the distance entirely accurately. This was because my Chinese lady companion had started to sell me seriously short; the measurements she was providing were all significantly understated and were to collapse altogether within the next 24 hours. I thought this was a real pity. I felt the Chinese lady had rather let me down. I'd shown her off, introduced her to all my friends, looked after her with loving care and attention and followed all her instructions. And this was all the thanks I got. It seemed that pedometers and I were just not made for each other.

So it was Saturday night. It was Roche. I had a meal and a couple of good pints of Everards Buddings bitter at the Rock Inn and then wondered how I was going to spend the rest of the evening. Even its proudest citizens could not claim that Roche is a particularly lively place and I have to confess I admitted defeat and passed the rest of the time catching up with the laundry. Travelling light, especially with only two pairs of underpants, means constant activity on the laundry front, but even at this very early stage of the walk, enthusiasm was rapidly diminishing. It was certainly a solitary and uninspiring way of spending the first Saturday night on the road. The loneliness of the long-distance walker.

I did wonder how the Rock Inn came to be selling Everards beers which are brewed in far distant Leicestershire. Not that I minded. Buddings, I later discovered, is one of Everards' Seasonal ales. It is apparently brewed in April and May 'to reflect the spirit of spring. The hints of summer fruits let you know that longer days are not far away.' It allegedly has a 'dry earthy nature and a fresh sharp finish'. I thought it was quite gluggable.

After the industrial landscapes of Saturday the Sabbath saw a return to Cornwall's more bucolic and picturesque scenery. I followed the lanes north-eastwards across the A30 to Boscarne. My plan was to take the Camel Trail, a disused railway and now a cycle track, up the valley of the River Camel. I was aiming for the village of St Breward, a

23

settlement on the edge of Bodmin Moor, which would be my launch-pad for the crossing of the moor itself the following day. What I hadn't realized was that the railway was not yet entirely disused. I arrived at Boscarne to find a station – the western terminus of the Bodmin and Wenford Steam Railway. I looked at the timetable and was delighted to see that the railway was fully operational on Sundays during the month of April. Even better, there was a train due in five minutes. This duly arrived on time pulled by an extremely photogenic ex-Great Western tank engine (No 5552). As it hove into view my eye was drawn to a figure running – nay sprinting – along the path in the distance, obviously keen to see the train before it departed. As the figure got nearer I could see that it was carrying a very large rucksack and was, if anything, accelerating. It was Roy. When he reached me he wasn't even out of breath.

So another emotional reunion with Roy and Maureen and lots of photographs of the train. I had been careful to ensure that we stayed in touch during this phase of the walk, had cunningly discovered from them where they planned to stay the night in St Breward and then booked in at the same place. This meant that I would be able to set out with them the next morning, which was good news because I really didn't relish the prospect of crossing Bodmin Moor alone. Surely, in the company of two such experienced and professional walkers, I couldn't go wrong.

Given their significantly faster pace they moved ahead, leaving me to misread my map completely and make an unscheduled detour into Bodmin. Actually, I didn't misread the map. The truth is I didn't look at it at all. Having arrived on the Camel Trail, I became utterly complacent and failed to realize that it had a short spur which went directly into Bodmin town centre. It was Roy's fault really. He'd commented that the afternoon's walking would be good because, being on the trail, we wouldn't need to consult our maps.

Naturally I deferred to his infinitely greater knowledge and professionalism on the subject.

The detour wasn't actually much of an inconvenience, firstly because it was quite short, but secondly because I got an excellent view of Bodmin Gaol. This must surely rank as one of the grimmest buildings ever devised and erected by humankind. It was an urban version of Dartmoor Prison but much, much grimmer. It was just very … grim. The south-west of England seems to specialize in this sort of thing.

Back on the correct part of the Camel Trail, I stopped for the first Sunday lunch of the trip. I hadn't made any particular concessions to the occasion from a culinary point of view – I think the meal was the usual prosaic sandwiches and biscuits, supplemented by a croissant that I'd stolen from the B&B in Roche. I had, however, got the Sunday papers. To be accurate, one paper – the *News of the World*. I'd bought it that morning in Roche for two reasons. Firstly it was much easier to squeeze into the rucksack than one of the Sunday heavies, but secondly, and importantly, I wanted to mix my sources of information as I walked the length of the country, to view the news from a variety of perspectives.

And we were talking real news here. I brought myself right up to date on the activities of 'Princess Pushy' (aka Princess Michael of Kent) and her toy boy. There was also a feature on an extremely attractive young lady whose training for the upcoming London marathon seemed to consist largely of sex 'romps'. (I checked in the paper a fortnight later after the race but couldn't find any reference as to how successful these methods had proved.)

The Camel Trail is the former Bodmin and Wadebridge Railway which used to bring sand from the river estuary up to the farms inland. In the opposite direction the line was used by trippers heading for the beaches of North Cornwall. Apparently, special trains were laid on for the thousands who wanted to watch the last public execution in Britain, which occurred at Bodmin Gaol in 1909 when 24-year-old William Hampton was hanged for murder. The line was closed to passenger traffic in 1967 and was shut down altogether in 1984. Nowadays the Camel Trail doubles as my new-found friend National Cycle Route 3, and after lunch it was exceptionally pleasant and easy going along the wooded river bank.

The B&B in St Breward boasted a terrace where I sat with Roy and Maureen drinking tea and enjoying the spectacular views westward towards Padstow and the Camel estuary. Jane, our affable hostess, takes a great interest in her guests and runs an excellent B&B. Her hospitality that Sunday evening was warm in the extreme. She is a Liverpudlian and her husband is a former IT consultant who had tired of the City of London and decided to come to work as a plumber in Cornwall ... Like one does. Result: happiness. He was particularly happy on the day of our visit because his football team, West Ham United, were in the process of winning their FA Cup semi-final.

Jane made a donation to the NSPCC and the following morning produced the first kippers of the walk. If there was a nationwide grading system for B&Bs Jane would score very highly. I thought she might talk to Carlsberg. 'Carlsberg don't do B&Bs but if they did ...'

Later in the evening Roy, Maureen and I repaired to The Old Inn where we sampled Sharp's Eden (I was already quite familiar with the Doom Bar) and plotted our crossing of Bodmin Moor on the morrow.

'What a f****** day.' The first words of my audio-log entry on the evening of Monday 24 April. The voice drips with fatigue. The entry was dictated in Launceston. It had indeed been quite a day – and part of it was down to Andrew McCloy. Well, a small part anyway.

I have a great regard for Andrew McCloy. I'm confident

that any Land's End–John O'Groats walker, actual or potential, will at least have heard of McCloy's books on the subject of the end-to-end walk. Most will have read them. I personally find his work clear, accurate and informative. McCloy is a 'route consultant' for national charity walks and Land's End–John O'Groats is his speciality. He's written two books on the end-to-end walk. The first dates back to 1994 and goes into great detail on three possible routes including, enigmatically, a trail through the East of England, taking in such diverse locations as Luton, Thetford and Peterborough. The more recent book, published in 2002, is shorter and settles on one preferred route, although it does give alternatives. It's very concise with excellent graphics and lots of photographs. If there's one book that would happily serve all the requirements of the aspiring end-to-ender, this is the one. But there's more to McCloy than this. He's written books on subjects other than walking, lists pubs as one of his interests and is an Independent Local Councillor in the Derbyshire Dales. He's clearly a pillar of his local community and a very worthy, all-round, good egg.

Despite all this, if Andrew McCloy tells you there's a path over Bodmin Moor, don't believe him. Roy, Maureen and I canvassed a good cross-section of views in St Breward about the route over the moor. We discussed it in the village shop, we asked Jane and we had a long conversation with a diverse cast of characters in the pub. I'd also bought a detailed 1 : 25 000 map specially for the occasion. According to the map, the path took you on to the moor but then stopped and left you to your own devices. The bottom line of our discussions with the locals was hazy and equivocal but didn't provide any more evidence of a foolproof route over the moor. This may have been because the sons and daughters of St Breward, quite sensibly, had never ventured on to the moor in their lives, but were loath to confess this to a random troupe of eccentric Mancunians. Who knows?

McCloy's book, on the other hand, made it all sound enticingly straightforward. There was talk of a 'popular path' and a 'long north-south field boundary'. Above all, he seemed very keen that we should climb Brown Willy. Maybe this was because of its splendid name ('I was on top of Brown Willy today' is an interesting opening conversational gambit) but I suppose the more likely reason is that it's the highest point in Cornwall and Andrew, God bless him, very kindly wanted us to enjoy the view. While I'm sure Andrew's motives were of the highest order, we just couldn't get his directions to agree with the actual topography of the ground we were covering.

Bodmin Moor isn't particularly high. Brown Willy itself, the highest elevation, is a relatively modest 1,377 feet. Although we'd been able to see the moor coming for a day or two, it would be an exaggeration to say it 'looms'. But it is very bleak and inhospitable, and when Roy, Maureen and I climbed out of St Breward that Monday morning and got on to the moor our only basic ambition was to get off it again as quickly as possible. We were only up there at all because the alternative route was far too long to contemplate. The trouble was that even the most direct route was confronting us with a 23-mile walk to Launceston. McCloy's insistence that we add an assault of Brown Willy to this would have sent the day's mileage into the stratosphere. We therefore tried to edge south of Brown Willy in the general direction of the A30 and Daphne du Maurier's famous Jamaica Inn. The paths very soon gave out and we started to stumble around in patchy bogland. I fell over once but the landing was soft and no damage was done. There were streams up there and, strangely, walls and fences too, all of which made navigating in a straight line quite difficult. Andrew McCloy's book was about as much use as a chocolate teapot.

The weather was the saving grace. It was dry and clear. In rain and low visibility I wouldn't have fancied it at all. And I had the ace of spades in my hand – a compass. Every end-to-end pundit (of which there are many) produces an inventory of 'essential' equipment, and a compass always figures prominently on the list. I wasn't entirely convinced but thought I ought to defer to the pundits' greater wisdom. I felt sullen about this and very reluctant to spend money on a potentially redundant item. Eventually, in amongst all the whizzo equipment in one of Norwich's more prestigious outdoor shops, I happened upon a child's compass. It was labelled 'Wannabe Explorer' and had a fetching and colourful tape to put round the neck. The clincher was the cost – only £2.99.

I gave the Wannabe Explorer its first outing on Bodmin Moor, and while the needle seemed to wobble erratically through a 90-degree arc, it gave us a rough idea of where we ought to be heading. The gratifying thing was that Roy didn't appear to have a compass with him at all – not even a Wannabe Explorer. Maybe Bodmin Moor just wasn't challenging enough to merit a compass for a man of his calibre. In any event, for once, I didn't feel like a complete amateur. With the aid of some native intelligence, basic British humour and back-up from the Wannabe Explorer, we edged in approximately the right direction.

The good thing about Bodmin Moor is that it isn't very big, and before lunch we could see our way down. We ate our sandwiches at Blackhill Farm and then pressed on across the eastern edge of the moor to Westmoorgate.

By the time we got there we'd done the hard work, but there was still a long way to go to Launceston. It was a beautiful walk, ending with the lane that runs along the Kensey valley parallel with the Launceston Steam Railway. But by the time we got to the outskirts of Launceston I was beyond fatigue – little suspecting that the unkindest cut of all was still to come. Most towns lie in valleys, and the normal finale to a day's walking comprises a gradual and grateful descent to journey's end. Launceston is the exception that proves the rule. The town nestles by the castle which sits astride a large natural mound dominating the surrounding countryside. To make matters even worse our B&B in Highfield Park Road was almost as high as Brown Willy.

I wouldn't call what I did that night 'eating and drinking'. I think the most accurate term would be 'ingesting'. In the same way that a jet engine sucks in birds, runway debris – indeed anything in its path – with total indiscrimination, my mouth took in whatever my hands could lift in its general direction. It must have been appalling to watch. We hit the Eden Ale again and then adjourned to a fish-and-chip bar whose (lady) manager had won the 2005 Young Chip Shop Manager of the Year award. When I'd finished my food my hands merely transferred their attention to Maureen's plate and continued their remorseless shovelling of food. It was all entirely involuntary. Fortunately Maureen didn't seem to mind. I don't think I've ever been so tired or so hungry.

Sharp's Eden Ale, incidentally, is a 'natural' beer brewed 'in conjunction with the Eden Project' and 'in conscience with the environment'. I just thought I'd pass that on for what it's worth. Quite honestly, I think I preferred the Doom Bar. Also, I was very sorry that I couldn't devote more time or mental energy to the chip-shop lady but, quite frankly, I was beyond help.

Monday's 23 miles brought the total distance covered since Land's End to exactly 100. It was a landmark, and the next morning would bring another – the first change of county.

I'd also be saying goodbye to Roy and Maureen. They were aiming for Okehampton, some 24 miles distant. I considered this way too ambitious after Monday's exertions and had set my sights on Bridestowe, 'only' 17 miles away.

We'd agreed that we'd get ourselves out of Launceston and then say our farewells. I'd somehow acquired a guidebook to the Two Castles Way – a trail between Launceston and Okehampton – which instructed us how to extricate ourselves quickly and effectively from Launceston. Once we'd done this there was no point in Roy and Maureen sticking around and adapting their natural pace to that of a comparative tortoise. They covered the ground so quickly (and my natural pace was so slow) that the only sensible solution was to confront reality and agree to a parting of the ways. The convoy system – i.e. moving at the pace of the slowest ship – was neither necessary nor desirable, particularly as we had no more Bodmin Moors to cross.

So we walked past the castle, under the Southgate Arch and back down the steep hill to the valley of the River Kensey. After the valedictions Roy and Maureen pulled rapidly away. Maureen had little woollen Noddy and Big Ears dolls attached to her rucksack which bounced up and down as she walked. They were soon out of sight.

I wondered if I'd see Roy and Maureen again. I'd only known them for four days but (in the best possible sense) it felt like forever. They had been a terrific help over the last few days, providing superb company, radiating confidence and dispensing unlimited kindness and assistance to the novice walker (me). Their generosity knew no bounds. It included an offer to use their house near Burnley in Lancashire if my route took me in the vicinity – a gesture that was entirely typical of two remarkable people. Retired, the list of their various sporting and community involvements is endless. Maureen has an MBE for services to the Girl Guide movement.

I followed the lane to Polson Bridge where I crossed the River Tamar into Devon. After six days, finally, another county. Having also clocked up the century of miles, I was starting to feel altogether more sanguine about the whole project. When asked the question 'where are you headed?' during the first few days, the reply was usually tentative and diffident. 'Well, John O'Groats, actually, with a bit of luck' or 'You may not believe this but I'm trying for John

O'Groats.' These responses were invariably politely received, but there was often an accompanying scepticism, understated but discernible, and sometimes just outright amusement. However, I could now point to a modest but growing track record and was in a position to answer the question with a little more confidence.

And there *were* grounds for confidence. The body was responding well. The legs no longer twitched during the night. And the foot audits were revealing nothing untoward. I felt OK – even after yesterday's holocaust.

Given this favourable state of affairs, I decided it was now time to stop worrying. I felt I should relax, live a little and focus on what was going on around me. Because there was a lot happening and most of it was good.

3

I think I'd only been to Devon once in the previous 25 years and I'd forgotten what a magnificent place it is. I spent the next four days walking across the county and, in retrospect, they were among the very best of the whole walk. It had been a cold spring thus far but the weather was now excellent – bright, clear and warm – and I was suddenly pitched into the middle of an English spring making up for lost time in one of its most classical settings. Devon has everything. A magnificent coastline, moorland, mountains, fine historic towns, delightful villages. But the best thing about Devon is its normal, ordinary bits. The routinely beautiful lush rolling terrain everywhere you look. By English standards the whole thing is scenic overload. And that's just South Devon. I've never been to the northern bit.

And I had chance for the first time in several decades to actually take the time to savour the spring. The English language is intensely rich, not least in the number of words that describe shades of green. My thesaurus lists around 40, and you'd need them all to give an accurate account of all the wonderful fresh colours that were emerging along the route – each tree sporting a fresh green subtly different to its neighbour. I'd be pushed to distinguish between, for example, Chartreuse and Nile green or between leek green and emerald. My assessments would stumble along the more pedestrian lines of 'light green', 'a slightly darker shade of green' and 'not quite so light a green'. The springtime freshness of the leaves is soon lost, and with it the fine gradations of colour, but while it's there, describing it would stretch even the very largest of vocabularies. To make the mix even headier, many trees were coming into blossom. It was absolutely magnificent.

My route took me round the northern edge of Dartmoor through Okehampton, Crediton and Tiverton. Dartmoor is significantly higher than Bodmin Moor and covers a much larger area. Unlike its smaller Cornish cousin it has a distinctly brooding presence and does a very good job of 'looming'. As I walked eastward my eyes were constantly drawn to the moor on my right, but the views to my left were often equally spectacular. An early case in point was the magnificent northern and western vistas from the old London and South Western railway line (now National Cycle Route 27) before it reached Okehampton.

I was also lucky with my accommodation in Devon. My first night in the county after the 17-mile walk from Launceston was spent at The White Hart Inn at the village of Bridestowe some seven miles south-west of Okehampton. This was the first time on the walk that I'd stayed in a pub (as opposed to a B&B). It was more expensive than the average B&B, but the bonus was only having to walk down one flight of stairs for a beer and an evening meal. The pub distinguished itself by being the first I'd seen to sport a flag of St George on its exterior in preparation for the summer's soccer World Cup. (This was 25 April and England's first game of the tournament was still 46 days away.) And the White Hart had a very well-kept pint of Doom Bar.

The next night was, if anything, even better. I'd spent quite a while in Okehampton that day trying to organize accommodation, and with the help of the kind and patient lady in the Tourist Information Office I'd managed to book places for several days ahead. The one problem we hadn't cracked was finding a bed for that particular night. And time was getting on. Andrew McCloy's suggested route from Okehampton aimed for a village called South Zeal, about seven miles further east, but the place seemed to be something of a black hole as far as accommodation was concerned. At the Tourist Office lady's suggestion I called a B&B in Belstone, which was a little nearer. It transpired that the B&B belonged to a lady called Pippa. The cost of B&B at Pippa's made me blench, but despite my assertions that, by market standards, her pricing structure was ambitious, and the subsequent deployment of negotiating skills that I like to think saved my former employers a fortune, the gist of Pippa's response was an extremely polite take it or leave it.

Against such implacable odds the big, hard-dealing former commercial hero caved in within about four nanoseconds. I took it. And what a great decision it was, because in the end I wish I could have bottled Belstone, and Pippa's B&B, and taken them with me on the road to John O'Groats. The B&B was lavish in the extreme, with a palatial bedroom, luxury bathroom and magnificent view out over Dartmoor. And the hospitality was lavish too – from the initial welcoming cup of tea and cakes in the conservatory to the full English breakfast. There was even an offer, way above and beyond the call of duty, to wash some of my socks. It made me think of the Carlsberg ads again. Pippa told me she was thinking of giving up the B&B trade, but I sincerely hope she keeps going for a while yet.

It had been quite a climb out of Okehampton up the East Ockment river but Belstone was well worth it. It's high, right against the moor, and is the archetypal picture-postcard village. Its pub, The Tors, is an exemplary village local. The décor is nothing special but the atmosphere of the place and the photographs on the walls mark it out as an essential hub of village life. The Tors was first class, from the food and the excellent Doom Bar, right down to the barmaid's cleavage.

35

Strolling back from the pub to Pippa's in the gathering dusk, nearly colliding with the Dartmoor ponies that roam loose around the village green, was one of those rare but memorable moments when one feels completely at ease with the world. I felt inclined to stick around until Saturday for the dawn chorus walk. This was due to kick off at 5.30 a.m and finish with breakfast at 7.30. All for a fiver. I didn't catch who was guiding the walk but I can well imagine that, having got over the shock of the early hour, watching the sun rise over Belstone and taking in the birdsong would be a lyrical experience.

The weather during my four days in Devon continued excellent. On leaving Pippa's the route from Belstone to Crediton was bucolic in the extreme, and there were plenty more postcard villages to enjoy. I don't know whether Trundlebeer is a postcard village, but with a name like that it ought to be. Unfortunately – and perhaps illogically given its name – according to the map it didn't appear to be a sufficiently large place to support a pub, and I resisted the temptation to make a detour. A few miles further east, however, Spreyton, was postcard par excellence. Lots of thatch, a very handsome church and the sort of cricket ground that the MCC might use in promotional material to explain to unfortunate foreigners, most of whom sadly lack such amenities, the ageless attraction of village cricket. There was a pub too. Believe it or not it was called The Tom Cobley Tavern and I'm sure that, had it been open, it would have exerted a gravitational pull that on this occasion would have been impossible to resist. I stopped for a rest in the church-yard and happened upon a grave whose headstone was a set of cricket stumps. Not an artfully carved stone memorial but real stumps, quite weathered now, complete with undisturbed bails. The stems of various flowers twined around the stumps, and there was evidence that the grave was tended. Curiously, however, it was completely unmarked.

36

And it wasn't just the villages. I enjoyed digging round the market town of Crediton that afternoon. Its parish church, The Collegiate Church of the Holy Cross and the Mother of Him who Hung Thereon (to give it its full title), is a magnificent sandstone building. It, and the name of Crediton, are inextricably linked with the name of Saint Boniface who was born in Crediton in AD 680. Boniface has been described as the Englishman with the greatest influence on the history of Europe – yet his name is virtually unknown in the country of his birth. I'd certainly never come across him before. This is because his life's work as a missionary was carried out chiefly in Germany. He was created Primate of all Germany in AD 745 and is actually the patron saint of both Germany and Holland.

The church is also notable for its memorials to two soldiers, one a historical figure and the other a virtually unknown victim of the Great War. After Saint Boniface, General Sir Redvers Buller VC was perhaps the second most renowned son of Crediton. With a name like that he must have been destined for stardom from the word go. He was one of the most distinguished military figures of the Victorian era, winning a VC during the Zulu wars, and playing a preeminent role in many of Britain's nineteenth-century colonial campaigns. His memorial occupies a large part of one of the walls in the nave. However, I found the second memorial more moving. It was to a man called Harold Charles Organ, killed at Ypres in 1917, who in civilian life had eponymously occupied the role as the church organist. His memorial reproduces extracts of letters written to his wife by his brother officers after his death – letters which, in the restrained but staunch prose of the time, speak of a very steadfast and selfless Englishman.

There were more good villages and pubs on my next – and final – day in Devon, when I moved on from Crediton to Tiverton. I was particularly impressed with Thorverton and its pub, The Thorverton Arms, where I called in for morning coffee (only coffee – honest). After I'd finished my drink I went to the gents to discover, prominently displayed at eye level, a calendar produced by the local Lady Farmers Group in the style originally popularized by the Rylstone Women's Institute and the subsequent film Calendar Girls. It was extremely well done, and I gave it the time it deserved. Such was the length of my absence from the bar that on my return I found my seat occupied by members of the local art group who, having just finished one of their regular meetings, had quite understandably concluded that the previous occupant of the table had departed, and were now settling down to the social side of their agenda. By the time I'd looked at the art and explained to the club members why an ageing vagrant was apparently gatecrashing their meeting, a simple coffee break had become quite a rich and varied occasion. And without a drop of beer having passed my lips. The Thorverton Arms came across as another thriving and active local pub – an impression reinforced by my subsequent sighting of a poster advertising a visit by Eric Bristow, the former world darts champion, for a match on 27 May. That, I'm sure, would have been an excellent night.

Thorverton also provided me with the last of my great Dartmoor views. It was the point at which my easterly course turned sharply north to join the valley of the River Exe and then to follow it to Tiverton. Before setting out again from the pub I'd looked at the map and paid particularly close attention to the contour lines. This is something one never has to do in Norfolk – in fact I would guess that the average Norfolkman's grasp of the concept of contour lines is sketchy in the extreme. The last few days had, however, provided me with a salutary reminder of their meaning, and I noted with some dismay that on this occasion the lines were very close together indeed. I was therefore mentally forearmed when the road out of Thorverton climbed almost vertically. But I was entirely unprepared for the view when I crested the rise at about 600 feet. It was staggering – the best of the walk to date. By this time Dartmoor was behind me but it was still doing an excellent job of looming. It stood out, high, sharp and bleak to the west and south-west. Due south lay smaller hills which concealed the city of Exeter; in a straight line the city centre was only some seven miles away, but the panorama that most drew my attention lay to the east, over the other side of the River Exe. This was where I was headed and, here again, I could see for miles. The view was still stunning, but the hills were lower and the valleys flatter. It looked just as propitious a landscape as the one I was about to leave but easier and less challenging.

Devon had one final shot for me in her bounteous locker. Having come down into Bickleigh I joined The Exe Valley Way for the final few miles into Tiverton. Much of it was through woodland along the river bank, with the occasional detour into fields, but it was flat and contrasted pleasingly with the undulating country lanes of the past few days. It made for an enjoyable Friday afternoon but it also demonstrated the need for constant vigilance, even in the most benign of surroundings, and how, for the walker, prosperity can turn to imminent disaster in a frighteningly short space of time.

I really should have spotted the problem earlier. The first hints that something might possibly have been amiss were two holly bushes that protruded almost rudely on to the path, shouldering the walker off into the undergrowth. The way then narrowed to the thinnest of threads, becoming increasingly awkward to negotiate. The degree of difficulty increased even more markedly with two fallen trees lying across the path; I had to get on my knees and slither underneath them, encountering increasing volumes of mud and stubborn undergrowth as I did so. I think that even someone as obtuse as me should by this stage have been reflecting that national walking trails do not normally have sections that would make the SAS blench. If the penny hadn't already dropped, it certainly did a few seconds later, when what little that was left of the track gave up the ghost completely, and I was left clinging with my fingernails to the bank, a sheer 15 feet above the fast-flowing river. What should have been blindingly obvious for some time now finally became clear. Lulled by the beauty of the surroundings, I'd somehow managed to wander way off the (well-marked) path on to a completely false trail through the undergrowth. I had a choice of either going back or going up. Neither was especially attractive, but I plumped for the latter. And it only seemed to take a few seconds before I emerged, muddied and sweating, on to the broad, tranquil, sunlit highway through the trees that was The Exe Valley Way. As events turned out, this wouldn't be the last time I'd try to snatch defeat from the jaws of victory, after hard work on a walk had put me in a very promising position.

When I got to Tiverton I carried on with a routine that I had kicked off in Okehampton and continued in Crediton. I went to the library. The libraries were another aspect of Devon that impressed me mightily. In fact I became increasingly impressed with the quality of our national library system as the walk progressed. Tiverton Library was located in the brand new, whizzy, town hall/civic centre and appeared very well equipped. The staff were also unfailingly courteous and helpful. And this wasn't necessarily a given, because the ageing vagrant who'd gatecrashed the art group meeting in Thorverton that morning was now an ageing vagrant with very muddy trousers, unkempt, and who also, frankly, didn't smell that great either.

I'd come to the library to do my 'blog'. Now I'd been pretty equivocal on the subject of blogs. Most seemed to be flatulent and inconsequential accounts of lives whose occupants didn't have anything better to do than float banalities away into cyberspace. If other people wanted to waste their time on blogs that was fine by me, but I'd never, for one second, contemplated having a blog of my own.

However, as I prepared for my walk, folk started to ask me how I was going to keep them informed of progress. The question was particularly pertinent in those cases where people had pledged sponsorship. My own personal opinions on blogs aside, there was a value for money issue here. Having pledged precious money to Blease's nominated charity, people quite understandably wanted a few bangs for their buck. If the worst came to the worst, and a pledge had to be translated into actual cash, then people were understandably keen to hear about all the pain and suffering that Blease had endured along the way. And some kind souls had very trustingly donated money already. Was radio silence to be their reward? Regrettably, a blog was the only logical answer. So with help from my son I got myself a blog. All I had to do now was write in it.

I'd sat down two days before in Okehampton to write the first entry. The problem was I didn't really know what was expected. How much did people want to know? What did they want? Was the approved kind of travel blog just bald facts and figures or something with a little more inner spiritual meaning? It was tricky. I was quite happy to keep the world at large informed, but I wasn't sure I had the time or the inclination to be a latter-day Jack Kerouac. I sat before the screen for some minutes. If bloggers suffer from writer's block then I suppose I was exhibiting all the symptoms.

Eventually I wrote '*Have made it as far as Okehampton – around 125 miles. Never realized just how big Cornwall is. Most serious challenge so far has been Bodmin Moor*'.

I sat back with a sigh of satisfaction. Erring slightly on the minimalist side perhaps, but accurate, concise and informative. That was more than enough for one day.

In Crediton I didn't want to change a winning formula. '*Arrived in Crediton. Around 140 miles covered.*'

Possibly somewhat terse, but in my view an entirely apposite update to the previous day's more expansive effort. This was going to be much easier than I thought.

But by the time I reached Tiverton the first critical reviews were starting to come in. Blogs, of course, invite comment, and the number of comments was starting to escalate alarmingly, even though the blog was still in its infancy. My daughter was just plain sarcastic. *'What an exciting entry'* she wrote. My elder son was a little more constructive and helpful. *'Maybe you should weave in some poorly thought out riddles alluding to the secret history of the Christian faith to spice things up a bit. Some murderous albino monks might help too.'*

Clearly, expectations were a lot higher than I thought. It was not a problem I was going to crack straight away, but the standards of on-trail journalism had somehow to be improved.

I didn't worry too much about my blog that night in Tiverton. Other more pressing, real-world problems were starting to emerge. The next day I'd be crossing into Somerset. Encouraging progress, although I still had the usual issues of accommodation, route and timetable to consider. But there was another dimension. I'd also have to start thinking harder about maintaining on-trail discipline. Things like personal hygiene, lunch venues and the choice of pub were suddenly going to assume much greater importance. Life was going to be different. For next week all my comfortable rituals were going to be overturned by the arrival on trail of no less a personage than my wife.

Actually I had a few days grace. I'd arrived in Tiverton on 28 April and my wife wasn't due to join me until 4 May. The proposed rendezvous location was Bath.

So I had some time and some space to work out a plan that got me to Bath in reasonable shape. But not so much that I could afford to switch off. The first thing to do was to sort out a route through Somerset.

At this point it might be helpful, as background, to say something about my overall Land's End to John O'Groats route plan and how I'd put it together.

There is an unpleasant medical condition, well known in walking circles, called 'route boredom'. It's caused by over-exposure to conversations about Land's End–John O'Groats routes. The more experienced a walker you are, the more chance your immune system will have had to develop some resistance to this nasty complaint. However, non-walkers, or those with little or no interest in the subject, will find themselves extremely susceptible, as indeed will anyone with a normal, well-adjusted attitude to life. In its more acute manifestation the patient quickly falls into a deep coma and then incurs nasty head lacerations by pitching forward face first onto a pub table full of plates and empty glasses. Usually, however, the symptoms are confined to the rapid onset of yawning, sagging eyelids and profound fatigue. Treatment is simple. A change to a more rational conversation subject normally brings instant relief.

There is a related complaint, again mainly affecting non-walkers, called 'equipment boredom'.

To the end-to-ender, however, the choice of route is a source of unending fascination, and it occupied a surprisingly large amount of my time, both before and after departure. I started out with two inescapable givens. One: I couldn't begin the walk until immediately after Easter, 19 April being my earliest departure date. Two: I had an outer deadline for finishing the walk. It happened that my daughter was getting married on 12 August – and I clearly couldn't just blithely pitch up from John O'Groats the night before the ceremony. 'Hello! Here I am. How are we getting on with the wedding arrangements?' No, perhaps a month would be a decent interval to ensure my due participation in all the preparations. Also, and almost equally importantly, I had a ticket for the Lords Test Match on 14 July.

So I reckoned I had a maximum of around 12 weeks to do this thing.

Now 12 weeks is a long time, and initial researches indicated that most end-to-end walkers complete their journey within this time frame. But most end-to-end walkers are younger and fitter than me. In addition, what would happen if I needed a few days to recover from illness or injury sustained en route? And I would need rest days even if I stayed healthy. In any event, twelve weeks would be a hell of a time to spend on the road; even though people were planning to join me for parts of the walk, there was a danger of going stir crazy.

The more I thought about it, the more I focused on the need for speed. Well, not speed in its true, objective sense – the idea was laughable – but an approach (and a route) that would get the walk finished effectively without any unnecessary sophistication, adornment or self-imposed difficulty. Part of this, of course, came down to equipment. I'd already decided it would be essential to travel as light as possible, with no unnecessary encumbrances like a tent or cooking gear. But the essential piece of planning would be the choice of route.

The first decision was a formality. To the basic question 'north–south or south–north?' there could only be one answer. Cornwall in mid-April sounded bearable. The north of Scotland much less so. Would it have got light up there by 19 April? The weather would almost certainly be colder and less reliable in Scotland too. Getting there was also a consideration. Travel from Norfolk to just about anywhere is fraught with difficulty. The nearest motorway is in Amsterdam. But getting to Land's End would be considerably quicker and easier than to John O'Groats. No, moving north with the spring was the only sensible choice. It had to be, to give it the acronym favoured by end-to-enders, LEJOG rather than JOGLE. And LEJOG sounded better too – sleeker, sexier and somehow sophisticated in a continental sort of way. JOGLE just sounded naff.

It soon became clear to me that there is no one single approved or normal route. The permutations are pretty much endless. This was bad news in that I realized I would need to devote time to research, but also good news in that, as soon became clear, each walker can develop his or her own bespoke solution, choosing the route that best suits the requirements or preferences of the individual. So I set to looking at books, poring over maps and scouring the Internet. The dinner table was awash with paper. And I have to confess that I really enjoyed it. Yes, it does sound a rather sad activity, but do bear in mind that this work was being conducted on dark January or February evenings with the rain pouring down, or the vicious Norfolk wind howling around the house. Plotting a route through the Somerset countryside or following the course of a canal in Cheshire was starting to get the juices of my imagination flowing. Trying to picture the attractive real-life embodiment of what my maps displayed was getting me seriously motivated and whetting my appetite for action.

My research was telling me that many of the routes favoured by the professional pundits were not going to be suitable. These guys are genuine aficionados whose enthusiasm for their subject is such that they are constantly in search of the perfect route. And fundamentally, the perfect route is, within reason, the most scenic. It will eschew, if at all feasible, any contact with tarmac and stay as far distant as possible from human civilization. Now this is exactly what's required if you want an afternoon in the countryside, or even a few days on one of the national trails. The last thing the normal weekend walker wants is a stroll up the A9. And some end-to-end routes have been designed with the same

45

guiding precept in mind. I read of some that manage to avoid roads altogether for the whole distance and feel nothing but respect – nay awe – for the brave and hardy people that walked them.

John Hillaby's route was a case in point. Hillaby was a distinguished journalist and naturalist whose 1970 *Journey through Britain* is a fine work of travel literature in its own right – much more than a mere account of a Land's End– John O'Groats walk. Hillaby didn't disdain towns altogether, but the path that his journey took was pretty rugged. He started off on the coastal path around the north of Cornwall, went on to cross Dartmoor and carried on through the Black Mountains of Wales. The remainder of his route was equally rural. North of Fort William it was utter wilderness.

This was clearly not what I had in mind. So I looked for mentors whose approach more closely resembled my own. I soon came across a guy called Brian G. Smailes and ordered his LEJOG book via Amazon. Now, to be fair to Brian, he does call his book a 'Walkers, *Cyclists and Motorists* Guide' (my italics). However, it is written, quite clearly, from the standpoint of the walker. There are pictures of Brian wearing a variety of natty outdoor gear posing besides various land-marks as he hikes south. He's one of those fit, hard-looking, slightly intimidating guys (usually bald or shaven-headed) who make mincemeat of the toughest physical challenge. The problem is, though, that his route never deviates from the main roads. Anyone could have put it together in twenty minutes by calling the AA or visiting their website. It's no doubt fine for motorists and also probably OK for cyclists (although Brian never mentions the option of cycle tracks), but for the walker it would be difficult to conceive of a more unpleasant and dangerous method of getting from Land's End to John O'Groats. Brian's master plan for getting through Cornwall, for example, is to walk along the torrent of metal that is the A30 – a strategy so perilous to life and limb, it makes Bodmin Moor look like the proverbial vicarage tea party. If the traffic didn't get you then the fumes almost certainly would. To be fair to Brian he does go some way towards recognizing the problem. He dispenses such jewels of advice as 'Be aware of traffic at all times' and also suggests getting 'an early start at 4 a.m. [which] will ensure you can avoid some traffic for a few hours'. The usefulness of this idea is qualified by the insightful caveat 'This may be difficult in B&Bs'. Yeah ... thanks Brian.

So the £7.50 that I'd paid for Brian's somewhat ambitiously priced book wasn't the best of investments. His route was certainly quick but had to be discounted on a number of grounds, not the least of which was health and safety.

There had to be a middle ground, avoiding main roads between towns but making full use of them in urban environments. (Towns, after all, are interesting and add variety to a largely rural itinerary.) I needed to use national trails where these went in the right direction but rigorously avoid them if they didn't, and, above all, look for the straight line opportunities presented by canals, cycle tracks and disused railways. So, cutting the story short before the onset of terminal route boredom, I came to Andrew McCloy. His two books contain a wealth of helpful suggestions, and I give him the credit for much of my eventual route.

Between Land's End and Bath or Bristol there are two basic options. The long, hard way around the South West Coast Path, or the more normal route along country lanes with the occasional dash of canal and recognized long-distance trail. I naturally chose the latter. After Bath or Bristol the number of options is almost infinite, but I detected much common sense in the choices that McCloy set before his readers. By my reckoning the most direct route northward from Bath was via the Cotswold Way – 100 (obviously very scenic) miles to Chipping Campden in Gloucestershire. From there The Heart of England Way takes a direct (albeit flatter and less scenic) course between Birmingham and Coventry into Staffordshire where The Staffordshire Way picks up the baton, does what it says on the tin, and gets the walker very efficiently through the county of its name.

It was here that I started to part company with Andrew McCloy. Being an aficionado, the all important thing for him is the walk itself rather than the destination. Means are more important than ends. McCloy is very keen to present his readers with great walking experiences and, as walking experiences go, they don't come much bigger than the Pennine Way. This 270-mile beast is not only McCloy's recommendation, it actually constitutes the lynchpin of most other peoples' end-to-end walks. It isn't the longest of Britain's footpaths, but it's certainly the oldest, and arguably the most famous. Maybe people select it because it does constitute a substantial proportion of the end-to-end route and therefore saves them having to think about alternatives. It also has the virtue of being direct. However, it's also reckoned to be the most technically demanding – three solid weeks of hills – and the more I thought about it the less attractive it seemed. Reading the descriptions of the trail, even the names were uninviting. They all sound so harsh, spiky and unyielding don't they? Pub conversations along the lines of 'By 'eck it were tough up on Gritstone Crag' or 'I fell in't bog near Bleakrock Beck' had only limited appeal.

I therefore cast my eyes west of the Pennines to where a benign-looking series of canals draws the walker quickly northwards as far as Lancaster in a more or less straight line and, most importantly, along the flat. It all seemed a lot more wholesome and conducive to physical and spiritual well-being than slogging along the mountain tops. I decided to resist the urgings of McCloy and others to continue northwards out of Staffordshire to the Pennines, and instead plot a north-westerly course towards Lancashire.

There was, however, one major obstacle to this cunning

plan. And that, in a word, was Manchester. The massive south-east Lancashire/north-east Cheshire conurbation presents a formidable barrier to the walker. In particular, Manchester Airport sits athwart any potential route through the urban jungle like a latter-day Maginot Line. I could see why some might prefer the rigours of the Pennine Way.

But I had two hidden advantages that I felt might get me through. The first was that I'm a Mancunian. I grew up in the place and know my way around. Why, on reflection, it would be grand to revisit the place.

My second advantage was that I knew all about the Bollin Valley Way. This was the part of my cunning plan that in my view was particularly cunning.

Now while the Pennine Way is probably the UK's best-known national trail, the Bollin Valley Way isn't known at all. But I caught an obscure reference to it in a directory of long-distance paths, and Cheshire County Council very helpfully provided further details. The path starts in Macclesfield in the south-eastern corner of Cheshire and cuts across the county in a north-westerly direction, broadly following, believe it or not, the valley of the River Bollin. Crucially, and get this, it actually goes *underneath* Manchester Airport. How impressive is that? The Bollin Valley Way would provide the perfect springboard for entry into Lancashire and access to the canals. So the end-product of all this deliberation was that I now had a direct route along recognized trails all the way from Bath to the shores of the Manchester Ship Canal and from there to Lancaster. It all looked encouragingly straight and fitted all the criteria I'd laid down at the outset.

And when it came to routes I could now bore with the best of them.

4

The Bollin Valley Way lay some considerable time in the future as I set out from Tiverton on Saturday 29 April. I was aiming to reach Bath on the following Thursday morning, just in time to meet my wife who would be arriving by train a few hours later. I was hoping this would permit a modicum of recreation time along the way. Thus far I hadn't allowed myself much time to stand and stare.

Today was the first canal of the walk and it whetted my appetite for more. It was the Grand Western Canal, which I followed on another wonderful spring morning through Halberton and Sampford Peverell towards the Somerset border. Sampford Peverell sits astride the canal and is a beautiful little place. I stopped briefly to have a look around St John's Church and fell into conversation with one of the village's older residents. He asked me how far I'd come and initially greeted my reply that I'd walked from Land's End with enigmatic silence. After a lengthy pause he finally pronounced 'I used to like it at St Ives'. Far from eliciting admiration, or a spontaneous donation to the NSPCC, my response had merely triggered a bout of reverie on his childhood holidays. People still weren't impressed at the distance I'd covered. Maybe this would change when I got to Scotland.

I enjoyed a brief intrusion into the rural idyll by the main Great Western railway line. A Virgin train pounded past about 30 yards away, heading north. I'd passed this way 11 days ago on the journey down to Penzance and I recalled my feeling at the time – a mixture of exhilaration, awe and nagging concern that I'd have to walk back every mile of the way. Well, I'd done around 165 miles now, which was at least a start.

The canal originally linked Tiverton with Taunton, but now ends at Holcombe Rogus, a few miles west of Wellington. I lunched here in a spectacular deep cutting, the product of the decision made by the proprietors of the canal, when building commenced in 1809, to avoid the need for locks as far as possible and use embankments and cuttings to meld the canal into the natural contours of the land. It was a lunch of profound contentment in the spring sunshine. I updated myself on the current travails of the government. Three cabinet ministers had endured a pretty rocky week. Health Minister Patricia Hewitt had been received less than rapturously at the conference of the nurses' trade union, Charles Clarke's Home Office was in complete disarray in its efforts to obtain any sort of grip on immigration and John Prescott's extra-mural activities with a work colleague were inflating to epic proportions his already substantial status as a national figure of fun. My newspaper of choice the previous day had been the *Independent*, but I felt the coverage had been disappointingly sober. In its efforts to be informative, the paper had not really brought out the full spice and humour of the situation. To rectify this I'd plumped for the *Sun* that morning, and I was not disappointed. I particularly relished the description of John Prescott as 'a lardy Lothario'. Wonderful.

Even better, I got a text message from Ann, a friend who had recently had surgery for breast cancer. Her tests were clear – the sort of news that put the activities of a clown like Prescott into their true perspective.

Inept map reading condemned me to an unexpected and

singularly unpleasant spell of walking along the A38 (shades of Brian G. Smailes here – he would no doubt have been delighted) but it was only very short and I was in Wellington by teatime.

Wellington seemed the sort of place where income exceeded expenditure, but not by much. My pub of choice, The Eight Bells, was almost empty – strange given the quality of the food and of the Tawny bitter from the Cotleigh brewery, located at Wiveliscombe, just north of Wellington.

While my choice of pub in Wellington turned out to be excellent, the same could not, unfortunately, be said of my accommodation. This was a bank holiday weekend, B&Bs were booked and I'd ended up in a guest house. The distinction is clear. With bed and breakfast accommodation you're basically enjoying hospitality in someone's home. It may have limitations, but it will invariably offer a reasonable package of home comforts. The service will be personal and attentive and the food will invariably be good, solid home-cooking, often verging on the excellent. A guest house, on the other hand, is effectively a hotel. It's more impersonal, standards of décor and furnishing will be lower and the home comforts will be very dependent on price. Price will also influence the standard of food, which will range from adequate to dire.

I'd stayed in a guest house in Tiverton, which, given the price, was OK. However, it had given me an inkling of the potential downside. Its counterpart in Wellington was dearer – but offered accommodation of a roughly similar standard to that I'd enjoyed while backpacking as a destitute student in Tunisia back in 1971. Given that this was Somerset, rather than inner-city Tunis, the standard was very low. The room covered a total area of about seven square metres, with the addition of a walk-in shower that, given its size relative to my own, was virtually impossible to access. The bed sagged and the traffic was loud. On reflection, I bet standards in Tunisia have improved in the mean time and now comfortably eclipse those of the guest house in Wellington. There was a lesson here for the future.

I didn't fancy another Saturday night doing laundry so I hunkered down to watch television, and in doing so was witness to an event that transfixed the nation and was to be a major media preoccupation for the next month or more. I'm referring, of course, to Wayne Rooney's ruptured metatarsal. It was in the twenty-ninth minute of Manchester United's match with Chelsea that our hero went down under a stern challenge from John Terry, rolled over several times, writhing in pain, before being carried off on a stretcher. Even the Chelsea fans seemed a trifle bemused as the implications for England's World Cup prospects slowly began to dawn on them.

We'd been here before of course. I don't think more than one person in a hundred knew what a metatarsal was before the last World Cup in 2002, when we'd been subject to weeks of fevered speculation regarding David Beckham's chances of recovery from the same type of injury that had now befallen poor Wayne. To me, it wasn't so much the damage to England's chances that seemed the problem, it was more the prospect of endless ballsachingly tedious speculation about Wayne's recovery prospects. Only six weeks now before England's first game.

The next morning I had a pleasant and easy stroll along the West Deane Way, which broadly follows the course of the River Tone from Wellington into Taunton. I'd allowed myself a half day's holiday to mark the occasion, as Taunton was, by some margin, the largest town I'd seen since Land's End. So the day's walking ended around midday – an unaccustomed luxury – and I repaired to a café to look at the Sunday papers. I'd taken what I felt was something of a risk and gone for the *Mail on Sunday*. Not, frankly, my normal choice of reading, but I was keen to continue my new habit of varying the source of news from day to day. And, once again,

I wasn't disappointed. The main attraction, perhaps predictably, was John Prescott. The *Mail on Sunday* was keen to put flesh on the bones of the emerging story of the Deputy Prime Minister's indiscretions. According to the *Mail*, John and his lady friend would 'grope and grapple during the working day' in the course of their efforts to understudy Tony Blair. But, apparently, it was the disclosure of 'their encounters within the hushed nerve centre of government that would particularly shock MPs'. I didn't know that governments had nerve centres (and if they had, surely Prescott's office wouldn't be one). And why should the nerve centre be 'hushed' for God's sake? The problem didn't appear to be Prescott's extra-marital activities *per se*. The *Mail* seemed to have a lot more difficulty with the fact that they took place in office hours at taxpayers' expense and disturbed the hallowed tranquillity of John's office. And then there was reference to 'late night hotel parties at alcohol-fuelled party conferences'. It was priceless.

I must confess to a state of massive contentment as I sipped coffee and restored my blood sugar levels following the morning's walk. I sat in the sun and rocked with laughter at this prissy, prurient nonsense. But when I'd finished wading through it all I actually, bizarrely, felt a certain amount of sympathy for Prescott. Maybe the *Independent* hadn't been so bad after all.

So I had earned myself a free half-day in Taunton. This was, after all, the county town of Somerset. I now had to work out how to use the time to maximum effect. The problem was it was Sunday afternoon, which was not ideal, as the range of activities might possibly be restricted. Sure enough, Taunton Castle and the Somerset County Museum were closed. The town clearly boasted a large, diverse and apparently thriving retail sector but this was not my preferred field of exploration. I decided on impulse to see if there was any cricket.

Now global warming is a terrible problem but it does have one or two benign side-effects. While we all contemplate mass extinction we can at least console ourselves with the fact that we can watch an awful lot more cricket. In 1950 the English first-class cricket season kicked off with a game between Yorkshire and the MCC at Lords on 29 April. In 2006 the season had started a full two weeks earlier on 14 April, so by the time I arrived in Taunton it was in full swing. Although I'd never been to Taunton I knew that the County Ground was close to the town centre and quite fancied a quiet couple of hours contemplating another totem of the English springtime. Unfortunately, I was a day too soon. Somerset were due to play arch local rivals Gloucestershire the following day, but today the ground was deserted. Still, it was enjoyable to look around. It's a tight, pleasant and potentially atmospheric little ground set alongside the river Tone. One particularly homely touch was the job lot of old cinema seats that comprised the accommodation in one of the smaller grandstands. Somerset have never been one of the elite county cricket clubs, but for a spell in the 1970s and 1980s, when the team boasted Richards, Botham and Garner, Taunton was a fearsome place for opposing teams to visit.

By the time I'd done the cricket ground, had a look at St Mary Magdelene church (Simon Jenkins describes its tower as the finest in England) and done some advance scouting on my route out of Taunton for the next day, the afternoon had gone, but I'd enjoyed the break from walking.

I have to confess, however, that I didn't enjoy my evening anywhere as much. And it was entirely my own fault.

It was Bank Holiday Sunday evening and it seemed that half the youth of Somerset was thronging the streets of Taunton. Clearly not, one would have thought, the ideal environment for a lone middle-aged vagrant to enjoy the kind of quiet, contemplative couple of pints that he'd become accustomed to over the last ten or so nights. But a problem with my walk was that it was enveloping me in a kind of cosy cocoon where I was an amused but detached spectator of people and their everyday activities. For some reason, what was happening on the streets of Taunton and the corresponding need to amend my nightly routine, didn't penetrate my little bubble.

I chose the Perkin Warbeck as being a potentially deserving recipient of my custom that evening. The Perkin Warbeck is part of the J.D. Wetherspoon empire – in my view a potential, though not necessarily automatic, advantage. Now Wetherspoon pubs have their critics but, on balance, I probably come out in favour. The keystone is the large and reliable choice of decent bitter at honest prices. Close behind is the absence of background music. And, as an added bonus, there's the very negative attitude to smoking. All in all it *can* be a very civilized environment for the discerning social drinker. In his wonderful book, *The Longest Crawl*, Ian Marchant is, to say the least, equivocal about Wetherspoon's, expressing concerns about the 'shelf furniture' and labelling the pubs as 'cheerless temples to corporate Britain'. Ian's opinion is worth heeding. He clearly knows a lot about pubs and his book, while also describing an-end-to end journey, is written not from a walking perspective but from an infinitely more interesting drinking point of view. I can see Ian's point about Wetherspoon pubs, although I think he's being unnecessarily and sweepingly harsh. It all depends on your own individual experience. No, my only real quibble with Wetherspoon is something much more fundamental. It concerns the difficulty one can experience in actually getting a drink – especially on a busy night. For reasons best known to himself, Tim Martin is happy to spend a fortune on the internal and external fabric of his pubs, but then refuses to spend the relative pittance required to get the beer as swiftly and as expeditiously as possible to the thirsty and desperate punter. He insists on staffing his pubs with pre-pubescent boys and girls who do their wholehearted best but who are simply not numerous or experienced enough to prevent the onset among some of their customers of terminal apoplexy.

The Perkin Warbeck in Taunton that Sunday night provided strong evidence to support this analysis. I don't know how long I'd spent queuing for my first pint, but the length of the wait was almost certainly the main contributory factor to its almost instantaneous disappearance. Either that or there was a large hole that I didn't notice in the bottom of the glass. I was then faced with the immense challenge of getting a refill – and also, if I had the stamina, of ordering some food as well. I went back to the bar and, if anything, the situation had got worse. Everyone in the queue in front of me was placing immensely long and complicated orders, involving the 27 people in their party, all of whom, rather than opt for a simple pint of bitter, were going for cocktails of inordinate and mind-numbing complexity. The nine-year-old girls who Tim Martin, in his ultimate wisdom, had hired as bar staff, were doing their best, but it was an unequal struggle. I also had the feeling that the nine-year-olds were tending to give preference to the younger, sleeker members of the clientele, while the sadder, older, solitary customers (well, me, actually – I was by a massive margin the oldest person in the place) were not getting served as quickly. Across the crowded room I watched as the newspaper and pint glass I'd left to 'guard' my place were brusquely swept away to make room for what seemed like a coach-load of teenagers.

The odds were stacked against me and, if anything, getting taller. I have to confess that I then snapped completely and gave up the unequal struggle in the Perkin Warbeck, hoping for better luck elsewhere. Feeling ashamed, petulant and sullen in just about equal measure, I looked around for an alternative watering hole, but prospects appeared poor. By now the shame and petulance were being upstaged by something much more corrosive and urgent – a gnawing hunger that needed rapid attention. Just about the only establishment in the whole of Taunton city centre that wasn't bursting at the seams was a McDonalds. The need for instant gratification overcame the habits of a lifetime. I went in and within five minutes was sitting in front of an octuple cheese Big Mac baconburger or some such special offer. With fries of course. And a chocolate sundae. Within 15 minutes I was out on the pavement again. I'd had the instant gratification all right, but was now so badly digestively impaired that the rest of the evening was a complete write-off. I'd paid heavily for my poor judgement and ill-considered planning. I reflected that at least John Prescott had enjoyed himself, despite all the opprobrium now being heaped on his head. My evening, by contrast, had been a washout. It had not been in the least 'alcohol fuelled' and it had certainly not been 'hushed'. I'd just have to put it down to experience.

To get myself to stop sulking I subjected myself to a brief question-and-answer session.

'If you'd been at home in Norwich would you have gone into a city-centre pub on a bank holiday Sunday?'

'Nope.'

'Would you have gone looking for food in a crowded pub where the age of the average punter was roughly one third your own?'

'Nope.'

'Well, then, get a grip and stop moaning.'

One final word on the Perkin Warbeck. It was absolutely huge. With the possible exception of a hazily recollected Bavarian bierkeller, probably the largest drinking establishment I'd ever seen. The modest frontage gave absolutely no hint of the massive expanse within; I needed more than 100 strides to cover the ground from the back wall to the front door.

And a final, final word – the one pint of Exmoor Fox that I *was* able to drink tasted very good indeed.

I was up early the next morning. After two relatively light days walking I now had a 22-mile stretch north-eastwards to Street. It would be my longest day since Bodmin Moor. I was joined at breakfast by a man who professed to be tired as he hadn't got to bed until a quarter to twelve. I enquired the reason for this deplorably dissolute behaviour. Apparently he'd been – wait for it – 'showing his niece how to take photographs of antique furniture'. A racy evening indeed, I thought, but then, on reflection, probably a whole lot better than mine. *And* his stomach wasn't weighed down with an octuple cheese Big Mac baconburger.

The first few miles of a bright clear morning saw me back on a canal. I was definitely warming to what would be called in present day parlance 'the canal walking experience'. The Taunton Bridgwater Canal took me a pleasant few miles through Creech St Michael, the only incident to disturb the morning calm being a noisy confrontation between two dogs and a swan. The swan appeared, at the very least, to hold its own. At Charlton I branched off and rejoined my companion of the previous day, the River Tone. Spring was very well advanced now, most of the trees were in leaf and there were lambs everywhere. The Tone took me as far as Burrowbridge, dominated by a steep-sided hill rejoicing in the name of Burrow Mump. I crossed the River Parrett and continued to Middlezoy, where I enjoyed a very civilized and leisured sandwich lunch in the churchyard.

The going had now become very flat. I had reached the area known as the 'Somerset Levels'. This is a small parcel of wetland which has international status as one of the most important areas of its type in the world. It's home to all kinds of plants and rare wildlife, but is obviously also farmed quite intensively. The Levels are criss-crossed by drainage channels, and I followed one of the largest of them, the King's Sedgemoor Drain, which arrows more or less due eastwards dead straight for miles. It wasn't an inspiring walk despite the uniqueness of the landscape. The flatness, the straight lines, the complete absence of people and an icy wind combined to make it feel lonely and desolate.

I was able to make more sense of the Somerset Levels from the vantage point of Walton Hill, a narrow ridge that lies between the Levels and the town of Street. It was a clear evening, and looking south and east, I could see the Levels spread out before me back towards Taunton and the Blackdown Hills. North, just over the ridge lay Street, and then beyond, Glastonbury Tor and the Mendips. The view was a good reward for a hard day's graft.

And there was one more small reward still to come. I had descended the other side of the ridge into Street when I was accosted by three boys (aged around ten I guess) and addressed by their leader with the kind of shrill bravado that boys can manage when in a gang.

'Are you a hiker?' Not a promising start given that if he'd used the word 'paedophile' rather than 'hiker' it would have been more in keeping with the scornful tone of voice and the distaste of his facial expression. I confessed that I was (a hiker, that is). Then a slightly more conciliatory line of questioning as to where I'd come from, which gradually extended into an informal mini-tutorial for all the gang on the geography of the British Isles and the distance between the two ends. By the time the conversation got on to sponsorship, and that worthy organization the NSPCC, we'd been talking animatedly and cordially for several minutes. As a parting shot the gang leader put his hand in his pocket and gave me 10p, apologizing that this was all the money he had on him. Of all the donations I was given during the walk, none was more hard earned or gave me more pleasure.

Street gave me an early opportunity to rebuild my relationship with J.D. Wetherspoon. The Lantokay is another enormous pub – not quite as big as the Taunton branch – but close. It was a much quieter evening with less corresponding pressure on the juveniles behind the bar. One of the guest beers was Bateman's, a Lincolnshire ale that I knew of old, and it didn't disappoint. What did disappoint slightly was my newspaper. After the spice and colour of the last few days I thought a more sober choice was required, but the *Guardian*, while very worthy, was lacklustre and anodyne. There wasn't a 'lardy Lothario' in sight.

I was relieved to be back in B&B accommodation in Street after enduring the harsh regime of the guest house over the bank holiday weekend. And this B&B really illustrated the difference. Mrs Marion Salmon is a Scottish lady who dispenses punctilious but extremely generous hospitality, and she cooked me what was probably the breakfast of the trip so far. I've always been a sucker for kippers (and Mrs Salmon's were superb) but it was the smaller touches like the organic rhubarb and excellent lime curd that clinched the accolade. Marion and her husband, Richard, have a son who has completed an end-to-end cycle ride, so I guess they have a certain empathy with the concept. They certainly made me feel welcome.

Mrs Salmon's breakfast got things off to a cracking start next morning, and the day was enlivened even further by the lady in the convenience store who admitted to watching Ben 'Urrrr in bed the previous evening. My mind whirled for a second or two (what could she have been getting up to?) before I realized this was Somerset nomenclature for the great Charlton Heston epic.

Street is famous as the home of Clarks, the shoe manufacturer. But, of course, the manufacturing has long since been performed overseas rather than in Somerset. Street's only visible source of support is now the Clarks Village Shopping Outlet which, according to its website, is 'the UK's first and foremost outlet shopping centre and has established itself as one of the premier shopping destinations in the country'. I'm no economist but I find it hard to see how shopping can replace shoe manufacture as a town's major industry – but Street looked prosperous enough and it had certainly been kind to me. One thing I really liked was the draconian deterrent of a £1,000 fine for dog owners whose animals foul the pavement.

Unfortunately I had to skip Glastonbury. My route took me around its north-western perimeter but my eye was perpetually being drawn across to the Tor and its tower. Legend has it that Joseph of Arimathea buried the chalice used at the Last Supper underneath it. The brown tourist signs kept reminding me of what I was missing. The abbey would obviously have been a particular highlight as, perhaps more prosaically, would Knights Award-Winning Fish and Chip Restaurant.

I continued on the Levels heading north-east, a dead straight road (National Cycle Route 3) across Queen's Sedge Moor, until I finally hit the Mendips and immediately climbed one. I was rewarded with a view that encompassed not only Glastonbury Tor but also the city of Wells and its magnificent cathedral down to the north. No more complaints about the monotony of the Levels – out of Dinder there was another immense climb. Until today I'd always been hazy about the whereabouts of the Mendips, but now I had a very clear fix. I lunched standing up by a wall at Crapnell Farm, reflecting that I really would have to raise my game when it came to lunch venues. I couldn't see my wife putting up with the likes of Crapnell Farm somehow – and she'd be with me in only two days time.

Radstock was my destination that day and I made two more stops before I got there. The first was at the pleasant looking village of Chilcompton where I clocked a 'first' – a car trailing *four* flags of St George – one from each window. I paused to take a photograph. It was a small, dazzling white, sporty hatchback and the flags toned in so well they could, for all I knew, have been put on at the factory. The national

62

flag was now becoming an increasingly common sight on the road as World Cup fever started to build, but this was the first car I'd seen with four. It made me think immediately of Phil the vicar.

Our village church does not boast a large congregation. By and large the regular attendees tend to be few in number and at the older end of the age spectrum. They also tend not to be particularly demonstrative or prone to public displays of affection or affiliation. I was therefore surprised and gratified, on arriving at church one Sunday morning in early summer 2004, to find a car parked outside with the flag of St George hanging from a window. It was during the build-up to Euro 2004. Possibly a walker, I thought, who's left his car there for the day. But after the service I watched to see if it was indeed any member of our august congregation that claimed the car and was delighted to see that the person who cheerfully opened the door and sat behind the wheel was none other than Phil the vicar. Phil is an ex-miner from Mansfield. He's an excellent vicar in every respect. My personal view is that he should be Archbishop of Canterbury.

But seeing the white car with its flags in Chilcompton awakened me to the extreme urgency of the situation. Phil had better get the flags hanging from his car immediately, otherwise our World Cup hopes were doomed.

I stopped at the library in Midsomer Norton to make my first 'blog' entry since the avalanche of criticism that had greeted my initial efforts. This was a much longer entry – four lines in all – and I went so far as to confide to readers that I'd enjoyed walking along the canals. Perhaps I would soon become sufficiently accustomed to this medium that I'd feel able to make even more intimate revelations.

Midsomer Norton is the birthplace of the singer Anita Harris, one of my great 1960s icons – except that we didn't have 'icons' in those days. It also boasts a river (the Somer) that runs down the main street. I liked it.

On a more sombre note I spotted a memorial in the churchyard to the victims of a coal mining disaster in 1839. I had now reached the former North Somerset coalfield.

Looking at the place now, it seems strange that Somerset was once an important mining centre. It was never huge by the standards of other fields but its history is a long one. The industry was well established by the end of the seventeenth century. By the end of the eighteenth century the pit at Radstock was over 1,000 feet deep. There were scores of mines in the coalfield, many of them located in small (now idyllic) villages, but together they underpinned industrial development in the cities of Bristol and Bath. At nationalization in 1948 there were 13 pits left – the number had dwindled to two by 1973 when final closure came.

On its eastern fringes Midsomer Norton merges into Radstock, and it was here that I drew stumps for the night. I was staying in an old miner's cottage in another excellent B&B. This one actually offered me a chiropody session – very appropriate for an end-to-end walker, and the first time I'd had this opportunity en route. I should point out that unfortunately this was not a standard part of the service offering. It just so happened that Ann, the lady of the house, was undergoing treatment at home on the evening of my stay. To her surprise I declined the offer – the nightly foot audits had still not turned up anything untoward.

Ann Smith is a teacher and her husband, Mick, a retired builder. They had both lost their first partners relatively early in life and had met at a singles event. Superficially, I'm sure they wouldn't mind me saying, they're patently warm-hearted but unremarkable people. But actually they're very remarkable people indeed because together, in concert with their church, they had raised over half a million pounds first to build, then subsequently to maintain, a school in Bangalore, India. In his retirement Mick cooks breakfast for the B&B guests and spends a lot of time on the road to continue the fundraising. They had, of course, visited the school and over breakfast Mick talked about it and showed me the photographs. It is sad in a way that one of their major problems is the somewhat negative attitude of the Indian government, which erects barriers to the remittance of funds – possibly, in Mick's opinion, motivated by reluctance to see the country accept charity from a Christian organization.

Mick put some money in the NSPCC tin and I gave him an assurance that he'd get a mention in the book – if it ever got written.

Mick's local, The Frome Way, proved just as hospitable as his B&B operation. I was surprised and delighted to see Adnams on tap. Adnams is a brewery in Southwold on the coast of faraway Suffolk and, whilst I was aware that it is extending its reach, I hadn't expected to see it this far west. I was introduced to Adnams back in 1972 by my good mate Ed, when, as students, we were purportedly studying for our finals. Ed took me down to Southwold to get away from both the rigours of academia and the terrible Watneys beer that was all one could get in Norfolk at the time. The first taste of Adnams was like a divine revelation.

I rang Ed to appraise him of Adnams' onwards march but that night, for once in my life, I didn't actually drink the stuff. I preferred to take the opportunity of sampling local brews and went instead for the Butcombe bitter. This is a brewery that started out in the 'micro' category back in 1978 but that has, no doubt deservedly, prospered mightily in the meantime. In 2005 it moved into new custom-designed premises with a capacity of 40,000 barrels a year. No doubt it will soon be selling beer in Suffolk.

The next morning, Wednesday 3 May, was the first occasion I'd set out without having a fixed idea as to where I would stop walking for the day. I could, if I'd wanted, have walked as far as Bath, but my preferred plan was to stop south of the city and get myself some industrial history. I actually could have done this in Radstock, where there's an excellent mining museum, but what I really wanted to do was to look at canals rather than coal. Brass Knocker Basin (what a name!), the Somerset Coal Canal and Dundas Aqueduct lie within very easy reach of Bath city centre and I would have plenty of time the following morning to walk the last few miles and make the rendezvous with my wife.

Another beautiful spring morning and I walked north-east from Radstock along the valley of the Cam Brook through the villages of Camerton, Carlingcott, Dunkerton and Combe Hay. The names were all redolent of a pastoral English idyll and the places lived up to it, although all were home to a coal mine 100 or so years ago. The Cam Brook is rather more than a brook; it rises in the Mendips some way to the west of Midsomer Norton and eventually feeds into the River Avon south of Bath.

I encountered a little piece of industrial heritage earlier than expected when I joined a disused section of the old Somerset and Dorset Railway, now part of National Cycle Route 24. I lunched on the platform of the old Midford station in as bucolic and tranquil an English rural scene as one could imagine, despite the fact that, as the crow flies, Bath city centre was only some three miles away. The Hope and Anchor pub exerted the now familiar gravitational pull but I resisted heroically and walked on to Monkton Combe.

I'd contacted the Tourist Office in Bath to try to identify suitable accommodation in Monkton Combe. They'd been somewhat bearish on the subject and hadn't given me any leads. But when I arrived I was directed to the Manor House, which I was assured would help me out, and by 2 p.m. I'd done a deal with Beth, the lady of the house, for a night's accommodation. The price was way more than I was used to paying, but then again the Manor House was somewhere special. The original building was fourteenth century *and* I had a four-poster bed. I figured that I was now on holiday so

66

it was time to abandon any thought of a hair-shirt approach to life. Minus rucksack and map case I strolled the short distance to Brass Knocker Basin. I really did start to feel in holiday mode. After tomorrow's gentle 6-mile walk into Bath I'd have two clear rest days. It was time to relax.

Brass Knocker Basin is where the old Somersetshire Coal Canal meets the Kennet and Avon Canal. There's also the Dundas Aqueduct which carries the Kennet and Avon over the River Avon itself. Quite a spot for canal fans and I was rapidly becoming one. The course of the Somersetshire Coal Canal, at least in its final reaches, followed the route I'd taken that morning, taking coal from the Somerset coalfield to the Kennet and Avon Canal. The latter was a big beast in the canal world. It provided an inland waterway link between Bristol and London and therefore gave Somerset coal access to the wider world. It seemed extraordinary that, at one time, each of the villages I'd gone through that morning not only had its own coal mine, but also a railway and a canal on its doorstep. If scars had been left when all this activity ceased, they'd now healed completely. The course of the railway was still intact in places, but any last traces of the mines or the canal would be hard to detect.

I boned up on the Somersetshire Coal Canal – opened in 1805, carrying upwards of 140,000 tons of coal annually in its heyday – according to my calculations this represented traffic of around 15 boats per day – and making money for its owners until competition from the railway eroded freight rates. It closed in 1898.

The Dundas Aqueduct is a magnificent structure built of Bath stone and completed in 1798. The quality of the original stonework was apparently considered poor, necessitating extensive repairs, but it's still doing its job after 200 years. I crossed it and walked a stretch of the Kennet and Avon. It was all very beautiful, the only note of regret a spot on the bank where flowers had been left alongside a plaque carrying

John Donne's words 'No man is an island ... never send to know for whom the bell tolls; it tolls for thee'. I drew the inference that someone must have drowned there.

I took a stroll around Monkton Combe and had excellent fish and chips and more Butcombe bitter at the Wheelwright's Arms. No doubt much of Monkton Combe is subject to a preservation order. Personally I would have extended it to include the cleavage of the Wheelwright's barmaid, as it was so aesthetically in keeping with the magnificently attractive surroundings. I walked up the hill opposite the village in the twilight, the pale stone of the houses highlighted against the gathering dusk. It had been a good day.

I had the choice next morning of either taking the short route into Bath – northwards over the hill, three miles maximum, or double the distance on the scenic route along the Kennet and Avon, which describes a wide half-circle around Bathampton Down before entering the city from the east and meeting with the River Avon. There are, of course, several River Avons in Britain and someone had told me that we have the Romans to thank for this. When they arrived on these shores and came upon a river, they understandably wanted to know what it was called. For them, being Latin, and therefore logical, each river was different and therefore should have its own name. The locals, however, were of a different cast of mind. Given the fact that public transportation at that time was pretty limited, they didn't get around much and most people only knew of one river. Equally logically they called it 'the river'. The Celtic word was 'Afon'.

So imagine an exchange between a Roman centurion and a Celt.

Centurion (pointing to river): 'What's that called?'

Celt: 'What does it look like you stupid bugger, it's the river (afon)'.

So the centurion called the river in his locality 'the Avon', unaware that several of his counterparts around the country had done exactly the same thing.

The brightness of the morning and my growing enthusiasm for canals made the decision for me. It had to be the scenic route via the canal. All the fresh and subtly different shades of green were now suddenly complemented by copper beech, which didn't seem to have been there before. What also caught my eye was the large community of houseboats on the canal. One in particular stood out from the others. It was for sale, and there were photographs of its interior pinned to the hull. This was no rough-hewn barge. It had a lavish fitted kitchen and bathroom, and the master bedroom was done out like an empress's boudoir. 'The Leviathan'. Built 1899 and re-bottomed 2005. Everything clearly in good decorative order inside and out. Location not really an issue because that could be changed instantaneously on a whim. Yours for £145,000. Not having any feel for current price levels in the Kennet and Avon houseboat market, I couldn't say whether this was a snip or daylight robbery. But I wondered idly what it would be like. Sell the house. Sell the car too because you wouldn't need it. You'd just keep a bike on the roof of the boat like the neighbours did. And the neighbours would be interesting too – plenty of evidence of a variety of alternative individual lifestyles. It would be an excellent way of seeing the country – far more charismatic than a terminally boring caravan. Yes, I know that my wife is a gardening freak but most boats have lots of plant pots dotted around ... And she could always cultivate an area of canal bank. I could put it to her when she arrived that afternoon.

But there again ... Possibly I was getting slightly carried away with all this canal stuff.

I came into Bath past the impressive series of locks at the end of the Kennet and Avon and was immediately jolted out of my houseboat musings. It was reality time, and I needed to think logistics. My wife's train was due in somewhat under three hours' time, and having goofed off into the wide blue yonder for the last fortnight or so, it would be advisable to provide her with at least some evidence of advance planning, and to demonstrate that I'd given at least a modicum of thought to her arrival. I had at least booked a hotel for the night, but it would also be good to maybe buy her some kind of present as an initial peace offering. And what about a restaurant for the cosy reunion supper she'd be expecting? Also it had been hot that morning. I'd sweated hard and now smelt like a goat; it would probably be advisable to avoid looking and smelling like a complete vagrant when she stepped off the train. I wished I'd thought of all this before.

And I didn't even know where she was going to arrive. My Ordnance Survey map showed two stations in Bath, so the first job was to establish where the London trains stopped. This was quite easily done. There was a substantial looking station close by and one brief conversation with a helpful official gave me the confirmation I needed. That was one job done, but I was immediately stopped by a question from over my right shoulder.

'Excuse me, but are you interested in railways?'

I turned round. Oh God, it was an anorak. Everything about this guy screamed 'nerd'. And I was in a hurry.

'Only I couldn't help overhearing you asking about stations in Bath. There are two. The other one's the old Somerset and Dorset station. I can show you if you like.'

I was right. A complete anorak. But no problem. I could deal with this. I had a bit of an ace up my sleeve. I thanked him, declined his kind offer of assistance and then played my ace by mentioning that I'd actually had lunch on the old Somerset and Dorset railway the day before at Midford station. I appeared to soar in his estimation. If he'd carried on I could even have employed some retaliatory boredom techniques by talking about canals or the optimum Land's End–John O'Groats route but I was able to bring the conversation to a speedy and cordial conclusion without resorting to such underhand methods.

A little later I had got some of my pre-wife-arrival chores done and was eyeing a prospective lunch venue when I collided with the Somerset and Dorset buff again. It turned out his name was Barry, and we had a more extended conversation this time while he waited for his friend to show up for lunch. And when, 15 minutes later, our paths crossed inside the café itself (well actually it was in the gents), we greeted each other like long-lost friends and had another animated chat. Barry also very kindly fed my NSPCC tin.

I went off for a pre-rendezvous shower at the hotel, reflecting that I'd reached a very definite punctuation mark on the end-to-end trail. Sixteen days including today – and I'd covered 236 miles, an average of nearly 15 miles per day. The approach that I'd envisaged, the unspectacular steady trudge, had worked OK. I'd been incredibly lucky in that I hadn't got injured or fallen ill – in fact the body seemed to be holding up well. It was early days, I was still less than a quarter of the way to John O'Groats, but I was growing in confidence that I could do this walk.

Best of all, though, I was enjoying it. The weather had generally been good and the scenery in springtime south-west England a constant delight. I'd enjoyed the people I'd met and, although it had its limitations, the diet of best bitter and pub cholesterol had been excellent. And I was still feeling that glorious sense of liberation as I set out each morning. Everyone I met was chained to their home or their job and had a pretty fair idea of what the day held in store. I was much luckier. For the time being at least I wasn't chained to anything and my day was bound to be much less predictable.

And things would probably be even less predictable in the days ahead. At long last I'd find out what a Cotswold looked like. Would my wife enjoy the trail? Would the accommodation I'd planned be up to her required standard? Would her presence save me from the incipient onset of scurvy? Could I improve my standards of hygiene sufficiently to keep the marriage intact? Would Wayne's metatarsal recover in time? It was all gripping stuff, and although I now had the prospect of a two day rest, I could barely wait to get started again.

5

By day three of the Cotswold Way it was my wife's metatarsals, rather than Wayne's, that were the focus of anxiety. It had been a rugged day and Jane's feet were killing her. We were starting to get the hang of Cotswold geography. Basically it's an escarpment falling abruptly and sometimes viciously to the Severn plain on the western side (where we were), but by contrast showing a much kinder, gentler face on its eastern side (where we weren't). We'd been down the escarpment three times that day and up it twice. Gradients can put more of a strain on feet than walking on the flat and Jane's metatarsals were suffering. I'd had a peek at the guide book and, although I hadn't broken the news to her yet, day four was going to be even tougher. By my reckoning we had four complete ascents to look forward to.

But apart from the small matter of the walking it was fine. We were both enjoying the Cotswold landscape and Jane wasn't letting sore feet (and a cold thrown in for good measure) spoil her appreciation of the views.

And it was great to have Jane along. As I'd anticipated, the whole tone of the walk had gone significantly up-market. Jane's clothes for one thing. She'd set off from Bath looking like something out of a catalogue – gear that even to my untrained eye combined functionality with glamour and elegance. By contrast, after nearly three weeks on the road, I looked like a hobo. By some unexplained sleight of hand she'd also seemingly contrived to bring several sets of evening wear along. When I complimented her on her appearance as we set out for the pub one night, her airy response, 'Oh, it's just one of my outfits', left me wondering how she did this and still had a pack that was substantially lighter than mine. And in case you're wondering, I looked like a hobo in the evenings as well.

Perhaps the most enigmatic item in Jane's wardrobe was her sponge. Yes, I realize that a sponge is not normally a piece of clothing, but Jane wore one on her shoulder underneath the strap of her rucksack in order to spread the load and reduce the pressure on her collar bone. The sponge had all kinds of other uses on the trail and became Jane's equivalent of the multi-functional towel in Douglas Adams' *The Hitch Hiker's Guide to the Galaxy*.

However, the improvement in standards went well beyond clothes. I'd already guessed that Jane would expect high-quality lunch venues. Standing up by a wall at the likes of Crapnell Farm was never going to be an option. Fortunately, this being the Cotswolds, there were plenty of viewing points that met the required standard. Prospect Stile was a case in point. We stopped there for lunch on our first day out of Bath: a wonderful view back over north-east Somerset and the southern outskirts of Bristol. But what really floored me was the style and finesse of the catering. Jane immediately set the tone by pulling a napkin from her rucksack. A *napkin* for God's sake! What would be next? After Eights? Hot towels? Possibly even brandy and cigars. And the food went way beyond the normal cheese sandwich/Jaffa cake pattern that had become standard lunch routine during my progress through the South-West. We now had things like baguettes and even (sharp intake of breath) fresh fruit. The onset of scurvy was being postponed indefinitely. It was also good to share the load – both literally and metaphorically. It made sense for me to carry as much of the gear as possible and equally logical for Jane to take charge of catering and laundry.

The journey had also acquired a fresh dimension by virtue of a rapid and dramatic expansion of the hitherto non-existent 'nature notes' section of the trail audio-diary. I was OK when it came to things like bluebells and beech trees, but Jane was now drawing my attention to orchids, wild garlic and hitherto unobserved butterflies.

My two days rest had been invaluable. Following a day in Bath, where Jane and I had done all the things that tourists are statutorily required to do, we had taken the train to Bristol to stay with old friends Graham and Angela. We'd been to the National Trust property at Tyntesfield and looked round Brunel's SS *Great Britain*. From my own selfish perspective it was obviously good to give the body a rest. It was also good to have a break from thinking about the walk. There's a danger of getting too close to the minutiae of things like route planning and daily mileage, and the resultant narrowing of conversation themes can be extremely boring for others.

We'd returned to Bath on the morning of Sunday 7 May and meandered north on the first leg of the Cotswold Way to Cold Ashton in Gloucestershire (another new county – most encouraging). On the way we'd passed Prospect Stile, where Jane had so impressed me with her napkin. Breakfast on day two was memorable for our meeting Neil, who hailed from Wagga Wagga in New South Wales, and who'd come to the UK to look up some family history. He'd also run the London marathon. It turned out that this was his one hundred and somethingth marathon – he'd actually lost count of the number he'd run. I thought this was deeply impressive. We'd crossed the bridge over the M4, walked through Tormarton, past Dodington House, which is now owned by James Dyson of bagless vacuum cleaner fame, and up into the Sodburys (Old Sodbury, Little Sodbury). Jane eschewed

75

the opportunity of calling at The Dog Inn in Old Sodbury because, for some arcane reason, it did not match up to her exacting standards as a lunch venue. But her judgement proved to be sound, because when we did finally stop (at Old Sodbury church), we were rewarded with a spectacular view out over Yate and the Severn estuary and its two bridges. We then progressed to Hawkesbury Upton, which boasts a fine pub called The Fox, where we spent the night and where, slightly to my surprise, I found myself back on the Sharp's Doom Bar.

The weather had been mixed, but by the end of day three it had cleared. We'd gone through Wootton-under-Edge. Lunch at Ye Olde Swan Inn – my first lunchtime pub of the walk, although with Jane's 'help' I manfully stuck to Diet Coke only. We passed the towering Tyndale Monument and in the evening sunshine came down into the splendid village of North Nibley. But it had been tough. This was the 'up the escarpment twice and down three times' day and Jane's feet were giving her considerable pain. It wasn't blisters or indeed anything visible. The constant impact just left her feet feeling very painful and tender. And she had a cold and a sore throat.

We were staying that night at Nibley House, a magnificent Georgian building – now, among many other things, excellent B&B accommodation and home to the Eley family. We checked in and then had a look at Nibley church. I was also keen to go and knock on the door of the vicarage, with a view to being able to say that I'd met the Vicar of Nibley. Jane was less enamoured of the idea. Instead she gritted her teeth and limped with me as far as the Black Horse Inn, where we ate and I had what was, for rural South Gloucestershire, a curious choice of beers. The selection was between Kent and Cornwall in the shape of Spitfire and (yet more) Doom Bar.

With a night's rest Jane's feet felt better and the morning was a fine one. A good breakfast, a chat with Diana Eley, who fed the NSPCC tin: the day had started well. Jane pressed on. But the day's walking proved to be a real killer. Although at 13 miles it was one of the shorter days from a distance perspective, the route from Nibley to our final resting point at Randwick took us up the escarpment no fewer than four times. In its entirety the Cotswold Way gains and loses over 12,000 feet in height (although the highest point is only 1,083 feet). The numbers give a clue to the extremely undulating nature of the walk. Even to me, in my relatively healthy state, that day seemed to encompass the vast majority of the 12,000 feet's worth of undulations. We walked up Stinchcombe Hill, descended into Dursley and climbed Cam Long Down (which I thought sounded like something out of a Thai menu). The descent was immediate and precipitous, but not as immediate and precipitous as the next ascent into Coaley Wood. And all this took place before lunch. By the time we actually stopped for lunch Jane was struggling badly. She took her boots off, got the sponge out and started to apply some of the huge range of creams and unguents that she carried around with the aim of assuring her bodily comfort and well-being. It was like walking with a travelling apothecary. Of far more benefit, in my view was the refreshment we obtained from the Mr Whippy van parked on top of Coaley Peak. Jane sat down and gratefully ate her 99, but I wasn't sure how long she could continue to take this hammering. She wasn't interested in the Nympsfield Long Barrow, a Neolithic burial chamber, and there was no way she was even going to contemplate making the very short detour off the path to see Hetty Pegler's Tump. On another day a name like that would have been more than sufficient to tempt her off the beaten track. (This was yet another Neo-lithic burial chamber. The Cotswolds have more long bar-rows and hill forts than you can shake a stick at.) We descended again into Middleyard and King's Stanley before the final gruelling climb of the day to Randwick, which lies on the north-western corner of the town of Stroud.

77

Randwick must be one of the most uneven places in the world. I'm sure there are villages in the Alps or the Himalayas with similarly irregular and unfavourable contours, but Randwick must be up there with them. I'm not sure if the *Guinness Book of Records* has an entry for the football pitch with the sharpest end-to-end gradient. If it does, Randwick would be an immediate contender. Playing uphill, you'd need crampons rather than football boots. It would amaze me if any team had ever managed to score a goal at the top end. But it's not just the footballers who struggle. The village drinkers have it equally tough. Randwick has two pubs. We passed the one at the bottom of the hill and established that it didn't do food. We could see the other one and, even though we'd climbed a fair stretch to finally, gratefully, reach our B&B, this pub still seemed about 5,000 feet above us. It was impossibly far distant – way out of reach for Jane, who was at the end of her tether.

Our host, John Taylor, very kindly came to the rescue. Having established that the pub at the top of the village was also not offering food that evening, he drove us to the Prince of Wales pub at Cashes Green. Two pints of BOB (which I later discovered was an acronym for Brand Oak Bitter) from the local Wickwar brewery served to restore my equilibrium but the day had really taken its toll of Jane. For the first time there were allusions to her possibly abandoning the walk. We were four days into the Cotswold Way with still another four to do, and stoic and courageous as she was, it seemed cruel to ask her to continue.

She started the next day, Thursday 11 May, on the basis of 'I'll see how it goes'. And it seemed to go slightly better. It was possibly the old cliché about the darkest hour being just before dawn, but the route was a lot flatter, with just the occasional climb, and the feet seemed to be more inured to the punishment they were taking. We walked through Standish Wood, where even I was moved to comment upon the quantity and quality of the bluebells. We also took great pleasure in the view from Haresfield Beacon because it gave us a very good overview of the arduous ground we'd covered the previous day. More precious balm for Jane's soul if not for her feet. By the time we reached Painswick Jane seemed in better fettle altogether. We enjoyed the church and the famous 99 yews in its graveyard and had lunch, bathed in sunshine, in the courtyard of the Royal Oak in the middle of the town. We'd opted for an early lunch to accelerate Jane's healing process, which was fortunate, because shortly before our departure from the pub it was engulfed by a huge cavalcade of old ladies, who descended upon the place like a swarm of locusts. They were fortunately too late to impede the healing process, and we carried on up to Painswick Beacon where the views were urban – Gloucester below us and, to the north-east, Cheltenham.

The highlight of the afternoon was Cooper's Hill. The name may not ring a bell with you (it didn't with me) but I bet you've seen it on television, featuring as one of those 'And finally ...' items on news bulletins. If I mentioned cheese-rolling you'd get it immediately. Cooper's Hill has a gradient of at best 1in 1. There are parts of the descent, which is about 300 yards long, where the slope is 2 in 1. No, I've got that right, not 1 in 2, 2 in 1. Every spring Bank Holiday Monday thousands gather to watch contestants follow a 7-pound Double Gloucester cheese down the slope in an (often vain) attempt to catch it. The event has been going on for hundreds of years, but there doesn't appear to be a definitive explanation as to how it started. An ancient fertility rite possibly, or maybe an assertion of common rights. Who knows? The key point is the huge interest the event generates and the superlative fun it provides for spectators and con-testants alike.

Jane and I stood at the top of the hill. It reminded me of the view from the top of a ski-jump. It's not a terribly attractive prospect. The slope is too steep to run down but not quite steep enough to fall down. Whichever way you do it you get to the bottom very quickly indeed, and there's a fair chance you'll sprain or break something along the way.

I think the report on one of the 2005 races illustrates the entirely involuntary nature of most contestants' progress down the slope: 'The winner crossed the line after an uncontrollable tumble halfway down sent him way ahead of the rest of the field who were taking it a little less recklessly.' And it's not just the contestants who get hurt. There are also frequent reports of spectators injuring themselves by falling down the slope or getting whacked by the 7-pound cheese.

Cheese-rolling isn't just for blokes. There's a ladies' race too, and I was struck by the fact that for the last three years the women's title has been won by Dionne Carter from Auckland. Now it's a curious fact that with any extreme or ultra-dangerous activity you'll almost always find there's a Kiwi, either behind the whole concept or, at the very least, extremely heavily implicated. In this country we sometimes moan that there's a little too much attention paid to Health and Safety. By way of contrast, in New Zealand, they appear to have completely abolished the whole concept. The country now styles itself as the adventure capital of the world. For instance, when we lived there in the early 1990s, white-water rafting was a major attraction. Twelve years later, when our son arrived there during his gap year, they had dispensed altogether with the rafts (which are obviously only for wimps) and sent the punters down the rapids on what looked like small tea trays. And with every passing e-mail from our son the sports became more extreme. Bungee jumping? Routine. Parachuting? Yawn. We were relieved when he crossed the Tasman Sea to Fraser Island in Australia, where people routinely get attacked by dingoes. My guess is that the worthy Dionne Carter is actually part of a clandestine New Zealand government plot to import cheese-rolling, with the ultimate aim of securing for all time the country's leading position as purveyor of the extreme adrenalin rush.

The person I felt sorry for in all this was the bloke whose garden lies at the bottom of the hill. The 'landing zone' for contestants appeared very narrow, and almost certainly insufficient to cope with the speed of the various projectiles – both human and dairy – as they completed the course. I bet they come crashing through his fence and make a right mess of his vegetable patch.

You know you've made it in this part of the world if you're asked to start the races by actually rolling the cheese. We met one person who had had the honour of performing this august ceremonial function. This was Rose, the owner of the Haven Tea Garden, which sits right on the trail and has become something of a Cotswold Way institution. We sat and talked with Rose in her garden while we drank our tea, and she showed us a monster book of press cuttings on the subject of the cheese-rolling. As far as I could determine the worst year for injuries had been 1982 when a lightning strike had added yet another dimension of danger to the occasion and 15 more casualties to the general mayhem. Rose also told us that the local bin man (sorry, refuse disposal operative) would set the cheese rolling in 2006 – the event being then only just over two weeks away.

After we'd left Rose it was a fairly easy walk through Witcombe Wood to Birdlip and our B&B. It had been a much more comfortable day and Jane was feeling better. There now seemed to be a reasonable prospect of her completing the Cotswold Way – at which point we'd planned that she would return home in triumph and leave me to continue the trudge northwards. We went to the Air Balloon pub in Birdlip that night and celebrated Jane's renaissance. Oddly, once again, there wasn't a Cotswold beer in sight. This was a Greene King pub. What with this, and Adnams in Somerset, the Suffolk brewers really seemed to be on the march.

Fortunately, Jane's improvement was maintained the following day. We climbed Crickley Hill (another hill fort) and then paused to look at the Devil's Chimney. This is a craggy finger of rock projecting from the face of the escarpment and one of the major landmarks of the Cotswold Way. In the afternoon we continued on up to Cleeve Common, which is its highest point. For much of the time the weather in the Cotswolds had been hazy and overcast but today it was much clearer and we had excellent views over Cheltenham as we skirted round it to the south and east. At Dowdeswell we started a series of chance meetings with a photographer who was working on a new guide book for the trail. Jane was able to give the lady all manner of 'nature notes' advice, both solicited and unsolicited, on issues ranging from the Solomon's Seal flower to Brown Argus butterflies. I'm not sure whether the photographer fully appreciated this piece of good fortune, but it at least served to confirm the continuing recovery in Jane's energy levels.

We finished the day, Friday 12 May, at Cleeve Hill. Another Greene King pub, The Rising Sun, and more Abbot Ale. We now only had two days of the Cotswold Way remaining and, in retrospect, this final northern part of the path seemed the most 'Cotswoldish' – a succession of picture-postcard villages of golden-coloured stone. Winchcombe was the first of these. My visit was memorable for a rather tart and acerbic exchange with a man whose dog was busily crapping all over the pavement. With hindsight, I don't think the man was particularly impressed by my comment that it was a shame we weren't in Glastonbury, because there his lack of control over the dog could be costing him £1,000. I would have liked to linger at Winchcombe's railway museum (which was basically someone's front room) but it was shut and, in any event, not an activity that was at the top of Jane's list of priorities. I was compensated, however, by a view, albeit from afar, of a former Great Western 'Hall' class steam locomotive plying the restored portion of the old Gloucestershire and Warwickshire Railway, which used to run through the Cotswolds all the way from Cheltenham to Birmingham. Our second brush with the world of railways that day comprised various strength-sapping conversations with the National Rail Enquiries 'helpline'. We were trying to organize Jane's return train journey with the help of a number of willing and intelligent individuals whose only handicap was their (quite understandable) difficulty in empathizing with a rail journey from the English Cotswolds to East Anglia from their location some 7,000 miles away in Mumbai or Bangalore.

Leaving Winchcombe we climbed up to Beckwith Camp – you've guessed it, another hill fort – and had one of the last great vistas of the Cotswold Way, a sweeping view north to the Vale of Evesham. After a bucolic walk down the escarpment, Stanway was the next postcard scene, not a village as such, just a clutch of buildings around a Jacobean manor house. Our guidebook was dead right in saying that there's an air of feudalism about it. But it was incredibly photogenic – the manor house, its adjoining twelfth century church, a massive old tithe barn and a few houses. The manor even boasted a fine cricket pitch. Astonishingly, apart from inheritance, ownership of the manor has changed hands only once in the last 1,300 years. We ended the day at Stanton which holds the crown as the textbook Cotswold village. I'm often rather jaded and cynical when it comes to such claims but I had to admit to being impressed. The view from The Mount Inn must be one of the best views from any pub in England. (And the beer wasn't bad either – Donnington's bitter.) The pub gave me an incidental but gratifying little boost by identifying itself quite firmly as being in the County of Worcestershire. The clue was the excellent collection of cricket memorabilia. Worcestershire counted as the fifth county on the end-to-end walk.

I had been very impressed with the Cotswold Way – not just the scenery but the path itself. The trail was in an excellent state of repair throughout and was impeccably waymarked. It is maintained by local volunteers, who clearly give it a lot of loving care and attention. I'd also invested in a guide to the trail written by a guy called Kev Reynolds. This, combined with the ever-visible waymarks, made the Cotswold Way completely idiot-proof, which, I was later to find, is a rare distinction for any long distance footpath. Reynolds' book is accurate and informative. The prose is clear and well-constructed and, when moved by a particularly special scenic feature, it even makes the occasional foray into the realms of the elegiac.

For me, in a sense, these were 'easy' miles. My focus was on the Cotswold Way and trying to ensure that we both finished it in good shape. I'd lost sight of the larger end-to-end project and of the fact that the miles we were clocking up through Gloucestershire were also counting towards the end-to-end total. Without it really registering, I'd now brought the total amassed since Land's End to well over 300. It was only towards the end of the Cotswold Way that the wider context started to encroach on my thinking. After all, there's a limit to the number of beech-woods and bluebells a man can take. I began to yearn for a few tangible signs of the West Midlands – a motorway flyover perhaps or a few disused factories.

And the industrial heartland wasn't far away now. The regional television programmes were emphatically Midlands oriented, and we were beginning to detect a change in the accents we heard around us. So it was with a feeling almost of nostalgia that Jane and I left Stanton on the morning of Sunday 14 May heading for Chipping Camden, the official end of the Cotswold Way. We soon came to Broadway, which was full of the beautiful mellow Cotswold stone buildings, but different from the other Cotswold towns and villages we'd seen. Winchcombe had been very attractive, but at the same time a serviceable and everyday kind of place. Stanway was secluded and feudal and Stanton had maintained its privacy, despite looking like the set for a film. Broadway, on the other hand, had sold its soul to the tourist. In Broadway we couldn't even find an honest-to-God newsagents. If it was Cotswold teas, Christmas decorations or souvenirs you were after, well then no problem (although a rather terse notice demanded that you remove your muddy boots before encroaching into the teashop). But tracking down a newspaper represented a much higher order of difficulty. Even if you were looking for 'spirit organic hairdressing' then Broadway was the place for you. As it was Sunday the shop advertising this rather enigmatic range of services was unfortunately closed, but, trying to piece together what it was about, I concluded that it offered a combination of spiritual healing, organic food and attention to the old Barnet Fair. A shame really. I could do without the organic food but I desperately needed a haircut, and a little spiritual healing wouldn't have gone amiss either.

The final climb of the Cotswold Way brought us up to Broadway Tower, and another great view over the Vale of Evesham, before we walked on to Fish Hill, the Mile Drive, Dover's Hill and then made the final descent into Chipping Campden. Dover's Hill presented one final piece of Cotswold Way whimsy. The place is apparently named after Captain Robert Dover (1582–1652) a wealthy lawyer, who took it upon himself to organize an 'Olympick Games' there in 1612. According to Kev Reynolds, the games included leapfrog, wrestling, skittles and shin-kicking. I suppose it must have been a hairline decision as to whether to include the shin-kicking or go for the ladies beach volleyball instead. What a great centre of sporting innovation the Cotswolds have been! Dover's games were discontinued for a spell but were revived in 1951 and now take place each Spring Bank Holiday. So that means local sports fans have got a terrible choice to make. Do they go for the cheese-rolling at Cooper's Hill or opt for the shin-kicking near Chipping Campden? Either way I bet the Kiwis, having dominated the cheese-rolling, will now set out their stall to win the shin-kicking as well.

6

After a week in the lush and bucolic world of the Cotswold Way the next morning brought a sudden douche of reality. Like going back to work on a cold wet Monday morning after a pleasant holiday. Come to think of it I *was* going back to work and it *was* a cold wet Monday morning. To be frank, there was also an element of morning after the night before. Jane's victory over the Cotswold Way had been hard won and I was delighted for her. We'd celebrated very effectively.

To mark the occasion I'd booked us a room at the Lygon Arms, not the worst hotel in Chipping Campden. Not the worst hotel in England come to that. We'd made the most of the jacuzzi in the room, enjoyed the cinema-sized TV screen and done our best to explore the extensive wine list.

Now Jane had gone. I stood in the yard of the Lygon Arms contemplating the rain and consoling myself with the fact that if I didn't eat for a month I'd easily compensate for last night's extravagance. It felt like I was returning to my accustomed role in the engine room after a week on the promenade deck.

My contemplation was disturbed by a Japanese lady about one third my size.

She smiled at me. 'You Ingrish?'

For a moment I wondered whether, if I was standing in the rain in the middle of Tokyo, I'd be asking someone (who looked Japanese) whether they were Japanese. I thought on balance I probably wouldn't, but then realized that this poor woman had almost certainly spent the last week in the company of assorted Americans, Dutch, French and Germans, not to mention fellow Japanese. Seen in this light her question was actually quite apposite. I confessed to being English. We then had a very friendly but rudimentary exchange about the weather which went as far as our respective linguistic abilities would allow before quickly grinding to a halt. I thought briefly and wistfully of my Chinese lady friend in the pedometer.

Brief though it was, however, it was a very pleasant little piece of interplay and enough to rekindle the sense of liberation and challenge that I still felt on departure each morning. Who knew what further eccentric exchanges might come my way in the course of the day? OK, the yonder wasn't at all blue this morning, but even if it was a nasty shade of dark grey it was still well worth setting off into.

I was, in fact setting off along the Heart of England Way, a so-called 'Regional Long Distance Path', which runs from Bourton-on-the-Water in the Cotswolds to Milford, on the northern edge of Cannock Chase. I was joining the path some 16 miles into its course and planned to leave it in Staffordshire, just before its end. I very quickly realized that the whole tone of the path was radically different to the Cotswold Way. The landscape, for a start, was mixed farming country, flatter and more manageable than the Cotswolds, and the path was much more direct. I had a new guidebook too. It was written by a gentleman called John Roberts, and his prose matched the landscape he was describing – trim, orderly and unassuming with a nice, wry turn of phrase. Kev Reynolds' Cotswolds book had been (perhaps understandably) altogether more demonstrative and stately. Roberts' guide was cleverly arranged so as to fit both north-south and south-north choice of routes, and his instructions were terse and clear.

With all due respect to the Heart of England Way it's

probably not a path that figures on many walkers' 'must do' list of trails. Taken in isolation it pales into insignificance beside the Pennine Way, or even the Cotswold Way. Even with due allowance for the weather, which was poor when I walked it, certain parts of the path are little more than a mundane procession of muddy fields. John Roberts' endlessly repeated instruction 'go round edge of field to stile' didn't exactly set the pulses racing. No, the thing about the Heart of England Way is its location. The miracle is that it exists at all. It's a narrow and fragile thread of green picking its way through the West Midlands conurbation, an absolute boon to the end-to-end walker and, I hope, an amenity that will continue to be given the respect and attention it deserves by the people of the region.

Even on that first morning I could tell that I was making much quicker progress. I seemed to be moving more rapidly across the map than at any other time since leaving Land's End. Which was good, because I wanted to put my foot on the gas. My next period of R&R was scheduled for the end of the following week – some 11 days hence – and by then I wanted to be in Manchester.

I walked north from Chipping Campden through Mickleton and Upper Quinton, where I was given further encouragement by a road sign carrying the bear and staff insignia of Warwickshire. I lunched on the village green at Dorsington underneath the oak tree which had been planted by parishioners to commemorate the silver jubilee of King George V in 1935. At Bidford on Avon (another duped centurion) the accents were definitely West Midlands. I crossed the river and found the spanking new library with a view to taking one further step on the grand literary odyssey that was my blog. The computers were unfortunately all booked, but there was ample compensation in the shape of a chat with Karen, Bidford's lovely librarian, who was not only helpful but made a generous contribution to the NSPCC.

89

My exchange with Karen had been helped along by my new shirt, of which I was inordinately proud. It carried the NSPCC logo in an eye-catching, and frankly revolting, shade of green. Underneath the logo were the words 'Land's End to John O'Groats Walk 2006'. Not terribly witty or original but enough to catch people's eye and perhaps provoke conversations that might, in due course, lead to money changing hands. The shirt was the work of Geoff, like me a parishioner of Phil the vicar, and a long-standing friend. Geoff is a little older than me, and our acquaintance began eons ago on the cricket field, where Geoff was the much respected and revered team captain, and I was a young and callow debutant. We all called him Uncle Geoffrey, such was the quality of his leadership and his unfailingly benevolent rapport with his team-mates. He was the kind of guy whose advice and wise counsel you listened to with great respect when you were in your early 20s and I still, after all these years, credit Geoff with my decision to get married.

It was at a cricket match during a particularly dull passage of play that Geoff turned to me and said, 'You know Steve, I think you should ask Jane to marry you.' Jane and I were by this time already quite well acquainted but I hadn't given any consideration to the subject of matrimony. One of the reasons for this was that I was having far too much fun playing for Geoff's cricket team to entertain thoughts of anything that might possibly get in the way of my enjoyment. But here was an example of Geoff trying to ensure not just cricketing success but, at a much higher level, the psychological and emotional well-being of a team-mate. 'Why's that Geoff?' I said, anticipating a wise, profoundly serious and avuncular homily on the spiritual benefits of marriage in general and Jane's suitability as a lifelong soul-mate in particular.

''Cos she's got a superb pair of knockers,' said Geoff.

Be that as it may, Geoff's shirt (or shirts – he'd kindly made me two) had been brought to me by Jane when she joined me in Bath and were proving to be a great success.

I walked on through the rain to Alcester and stayed at the Roebuck Inn for the night. It was a fine evening after a wet day, and after a couple of pints of Speckled Hen (more Greene King) at the Roebuck I had a good look around. I liked Alcester. On the map it looks square and self-contained and self-contained is how it feels. It has an attractive and prosperous-looking high street and some fine old buildings – notably the tilting Old Malt House and the Town Hall.

The next morning, Tuesday 16 May, I continued on to Henley in Arden. A slightly better morning – at least it was dry – and the terrain was mildly undulating and more interesting than the day before. I succeeded in falling over twice before lunch, which was quite an achievement given that I hadn't done so since the Bodmin Moor episode three weeks previously. On each occasion I merely lost my footing on very slippery, but soft and forgiving ground, and came away unscathed.

I was starting to re-establish the routines that I'd been following prior to Jane's arrival on the trail. I bought the *Sun* and was gratified to learn of Robbie Williams' 10 day 'romp' with Tara Palmer Tomkinson. When Jane and I had finally found a shop in Broadway that deigned to sell anything as basic and workaday as newspapers we'd plumped for the *Independent on Sunday*. It had, to be fair, contained some good hard news but hadn't, to my recollection, covered the Robbie Williams/TPT issue in anything like the required depth.

I'd also, almost without noticing, re-commenced the Leslie Phillips impressions. These were triggered by the sight of any lone female who could loosely be regarded as in any way attractive, and who, crucially, was also safely out of earshot – usually in a passing car. All the impression amounted to, of course, was the single word 'Hello' uttered in a way as closely aligned as possible to Phillips' mode of delivery. I don't think that anyone, anywhere, at any time in recorded history, has succeeded in investing a single word with such a rich plethora of meaning and undertone as Phillips has with 'Hello'. My impression was coming along nicely, but there was still a long way to go. One of my attempts that morning was launched just as a passing cyclist appeared at my right shoulder. I think we were both as surprised as each other – me by his unexpected appearance and him by being addressed in a, to say the least, ambiguous fashion by an ersatz Leslie Phillips.

Henley in Arden is a stalwart little market town. John Roberts calls its main street 'a quaint, comfortable, harmonious mixture', which is about right. I had lunch on a bench right on the main street alongside the tower of the church of St John the Baptist. For a walker to stop and eat in such an open and public location can be a dangerous ploy, because the clothes and equipment attract attention – entirely welcome and harmless in most cases – but a pain if it's the village idiot who plonks himself alongside you. Being in the middle of a meal renders you temporarily immobile and unable to escape the clutches of the local lunatic. Lunch is ruined and you can't focus on the *Sun*. This happened to me in Harleston in Norfolk once, but in Henley in Arden I escaped unscathed. The town has two large parish churches cheek by jowl – only a minute or so after leaving St John the Baptist I passed St Nicholas Beaudesert as I continued north-eastwards towards Baddesley Clinton.

Before I got there, though, it was canal time again – albeit only briefly. It was the Stratford-upon-Avon Canal which links Birmingham and Stratford and maintains the interest of the walker by virtue of the frequency of its locks. The Heart of England Way leaves it at Kingswood Canal Junction and takes the short spur along to the Grand Union Canal. But the canal excitement was short lived. I was soon back in the muddy fields. It was a long day too – 23 miles by the time I arrived at the B&B in Balsall Street to add to the 18 I'd covered the previous day. Balsall Street has a rural feel to it even though it lies underneath the flight path to Birmingham airport and is only some 4 miles distant from Solihull.

I enjoyed the Banks bitter at the Saracen's Head in Balsall Street, as well as the hospitality of the B&B run by Janet Marshall. At breakfast the next morning I had the privilege of meeting her four-month-old granddaughter and had a long chat with Mr Marshall which centred on the manifold merits of the motor home which he'd built himself and which now sat imposingly outside the front door. It had the benefit of central heating and proper ceramic toilets and was clearly his pride and joy. He also spoke of the Meriden Gap, the narrow corridor between Birmingham and Coventry, how rural it is and how pleasant it is to live there. He was understandably and rightly keen that the planners should maintain it as such.

That third day on the Heart of England Way, Wednesday 17 May, began with a small domestic disaster, when my best pair of spectacles fell apart as I did my morning ablutions. I am desperately short-sighted, but no problem, I always carry a spare pair. It was to be another long (and wet) day, 21 miles in all, to Kingsbury. However, it had its points of interest, the first being the small village of Berkswell, about 2 miles north-east of Balsall Street. It's a gorgeous little place with an old hall, stocks, an ancient well and a grand church with an unusual two-storey entrance, the upper floor of which is used as the vestry. To my great regret I missed the pub, which allegedly has a Russian cannon captured in the Crimean War. Strangely, Berkswell is not alone in having an artefact of this nature. I believe it shares the distinction with Retford in Nottinghamshire, and for all I know there could be several others. It must have been quite the done thing.

'Fancy a souvenir from the Crimea, Dad?'

'Yeah, OK, bring us back a Russian cannon, son. Two if you can manage it. I'm looking for a Christmas present for your Aunt Mabel.'

Although I missed the pub I did get to visit Berkswell's post office-cum-village store. The lady behind the counter had lived in Norwich, which gave us instant rapport. She also said she could tell I was a long-distance walker, and not an ordinary rambler. I was flattered, thinking she must have inferred this from my purposeful demeanour and the steely glint in my eye. (I was practising the steely glint as well as the Leslie Phillips impressions.) But on reflection I felt that her view more probably derived from the filthy trousers, unkempt hair and general air of fatigue.

From Berkswell the path gained elevation, and the high-rise buildings of Birmingham were clearly visible over to the left. A little later, near Meriden, the view to the right encompassed the western fringe of Coventry. Another landmark was the crossing of the M6, which was immediately followed by a farm that seemed to me to be the absolute epitome of countryside squalor and dereliction. The place was littered with rusty and abandoned carts, vehicles and obscure pieces of farm machinery. It was like a rural Toxteth.

A little later came the moment that I'd been dreading ever since Land's End. It had to happen at some stage – you just can't spend days crossing endless vistas of fields without at some stage having a serious confrontation with some cattle. Now, fundamentally, I'm not good with animals. It's not that I don't like them, it's more that my experience of things like dogs and cats is very limited. And as for cows, well I grew up in Manchester for God's sake, so my experience of them is zero. No, it's not dislike, it's more a lack of trust – and, yes, to be quite frank, lack of trust can very soon translate into outright fear.

Two days previously I'd crossed a field containing what, to my urban and untutored eye, looked suspiciously like a bull in amongst a large number of cows. He was miles away and I was always going to be favourite in any race to the stile. But I was distinctly uncomfortable – a feeling that had been

94

replicated that very morning shortly after Toxteth, when I'd eyeballed a number of doe-eyed and dribbling cows who were standing hard by a stile, before I finally plucked up courage and climbed it. They'd continued to dribble and look doe-eyed as I walked right past them, but if I thought I'd confronted the worst and got away with it, I was sadly mistaken.

The climactic moment came as I encountered a field of bullocks, which I could see, as I approached, were of a manifestly frisky and energetic disposition. As I walked towards them across the adjoining field I watched them all suddenly rush off, as if summoned, in a mini-stampede to the bottom corner of their own field and mill around boisterously to no apparent purpose. Somehow, it just didn't look promising, and I hung around for a couple of minutes waiting for the whole situation to stabilize. The contours of the land were such that my position at the stile giving access to the field deprived me of an encompassing view of the all-important bottom corner. However, the few beasts that I *could* see had stopped milling and now seemed fairly quiescent. I was hungry and had a lot of walking to do. Although I still had a persistent feeling of unease I decided to go for it.

I hadn't gone more than 50 yards before I realized that the field was considerably bigger than I'd first thought. The stile I was aiming for seemed a long way distant. If those animals got their act together they'd easily be able to head me off. I kept glancing round furtively. At first they didn't seem to have noticed me, but before long they started to edge in my general direction. There wasn't as yet much cohesion or conviction in their movements, but now they clearly *had* seen me and were, at the very least, showing signs of curiosity. And the next snatched glance over the shoulder left me with a distinct impression of a growing sense of purpose amongst the cattle, a burgeoning understanding of the vulnerability of the intruder and of the heavy odds in their favour. There

95

must have been about 20 of them and they were now all trotting in my direction. And disconcertingly, I now noticed, some of them had horns.

Of course, the trot very soon moved up a couple of gears and within seconds had become a stampede. You didn't need to be a Euclid or a Pythagoras to realize that the angles and the distances were all against me. It was heavy odds-on the bullocks. Even if I jettisoned my rucksack and did a fair imitation of Linford Christie, there was no way I was going to reach the stile before they did. The totally inconsequential thought passed through my mind that the noise was rather like the Grand National on TV as the horses thunder away from the start towards the first fence.

I did have a plan for use in this eventuality. It was not a particularly cunning plan, and if it had been conceived and articulated by Baldrick, it would have been met by Blackadder with a larger than usual dose of his withering scorn. The plan consisted of exercising one of the two options open to me. The first option was to be trampled to death under the hooves of the stampede. The second option – and the one that formed the basis of my cunning plan – was to try to mount a kind of counter-offensive. I therefore waited until the Grand National noise was a little louder and then leapt up with my arms in the air, giving voice at full volume to a considerable volley of oaths and imprecations.

And the plan worked! The cattle slowed very considerably. A few of them even turned and retreated, kicking skittishly with their hind legs. After a few seconds they regrouped and came on again but this time the charge had considerably less conviction. A second burst of arm waving and more ripe oaths effectively ended the confrontation. They glowered menacingly and followed on at a distance, but I was able to get to the stile without the need for any more gesticulations or swearing.

I'm not sure what it was that turned the tide in my favour.

Maybe it was the arm waving. On reflection, though, I think the bullocks were probably so disgusted with the bad language they didn't feel they wanted to make my acquaintance after all.

The day still held one final brush with the forces of agriculture, although this time they were of an arable nature, and merely involved extreme discomfort rather than danger to life and limb. By way of background I should mention that, like 99.9 per cent of walkers, I try scrupulously to observe the Countryside Code at all times. A key tenet of the Code is the need to avoid damage to crops or to any component of the arable landscape. It must be said, that as a quid pro quo, the vast majority of farmers recognize public rights of way across their land and take steps to ensure that such paths are reasonably easy to negotiate, whatever the season. That afternoon, not far from my final destination for the day at Kingsbury, I came across one farmer who might have been an exception to this rule, although, admittedly, my troubles might just as easily be put down to an almost complete absence of traffic on that particular part of the Heart of England Way. Firstly, in order to rigidly adhere to the Countryside Code, I virtuously decided to walk round, rather than across, a freshly tilled field that was about three times the size of Heathrow Airport. The farmer should, in theory, have left space for the Way to cross the field. Nevertheless, I was willing to give him the benefit of the doubt until, what felt like several hours later, I came to the next field, which contained a mature crop of rape. Once again no attempt had been made to leave a small path through the crop for the Heart of England Way. This time, however, the crop was as tall, if not taller than a man, and there was no realistic way around the edge of the field. And it had been raining, or at least drizzling, for most of the last three days. By the time I emerged from that rape field I don't think it was possible for me to have been wetter. I was absolutely soaked. And there

97

had been a virtual word for word re-run of the deplorable invective I'd employed against the cattle.

I was not in great shape when I reached Kingsbury. Wet, cold, hungry and very tired. What I needed was the Lygon Arms and the en-suite jacuzzi. What I got was a room in one of the local pubs – accommodation, which, quite frankly, wouldn't have passed muster as an Albanian refugee hostel. Every single object allocated for use by guests (and the number of objects was kept to an absolute minimum) was of the lowest possible quality. This was indeed a place on which a lot of money had been spared. I should add, in fairness, that the price tag on the night's accommodation erred on the low side and was certainly not sufficient to create any unrealistic expectations. The place had been recommended to me by Roy and Maureen, who had passed by a few days earlier. Well, not exactly recommended. They'd discovered – and I subsequently confirmed for myself – that the range of overnight accommodation in Kingsbury was extremely limited, and that the pub in question was the best, indeed the only, show in town. Despite this elevated status, its range of services was not extensive and certainly didn't extend as far as food. I was therefore forced back out again in the pouring rain and eventually found solace at the Royal Oak, where lasagne and three pints of Banks bitter put a rosier complexion on a varied and sometimes difficult day.

The Royal Oak was clearly a sports-oriented pub. It was festooned with the flag of Saint George, and on the night of my visit was showing its patrons the final of the UEFA Champions League – a match between Arsenal and Barcelona. The Catalan side deservedly came from behind to win an excellent game 2–1. True to form, Arsène Wenger moaned profusely about the (to my eye correct) refereeing decisions that turned the game Barcelona's way, while conveniently overlooking the fact that his team's solitary goal originated from a free kick given as a result of a blatant and ludicrous dive by an Arsenal player. What a tosser that bloke is.

However, the big football news of the day – even edging out Wayne Rooney's metatarsal from the tabloid headlines – was the inclusion of the 17-year-old Theo Walcott in the England World Cup squad. This was a bold, even foolhardy, move from the normally cautious Sven Goran Eriksson. Only three weeks to go to the big kick-off and the plot was thickening nicely. It was like a gathering storm. One by one, distractions like the FA Cup Final and the Champions League were being swept away, and every spotlight was now focused on the World Cup. The volume of related merchandise on sale, even in the most remote and unlikely locations, was quite staggering. And most important, I'd passed on to Phil, via Jane, my concerns about his car being flagless. I was sure he would immediately have taken action to put things right.

I was hoping for a quieter time the next day on what I'd planned as a shorter (14-mile) stretch to Lichfield. And it was OK. The weather turned dry for most of the time, and I had an entirely trouble-free day on the agricultural front. Despite the somewhat unpromising surroundings, and the difficulties of the previous day, I still couldn't shake my usual morning sense of liberation and optimism. I had breakfast at the excellent, customer-friendly Lemon Tree Pantry, which made an ageing, rather shabby and unshaven hobo feel very welcome. Kingsbury had appeared somewhat nondescript, but I enjoyed walking through the Kingsbury Water Park, a nature reserve with a large range of amenities for outdoor pursuits. There was the pleasure of another canal, the Birmingham and Fazeley, and a sense of achievement as I moved into Staffordshire, the seventh county of the walk. I made a short detour off the Heart of England Way into the village of Weeford, and stopped to eat lunch in the churchyard. My eye was caught by a gravestone about 5 feet from where I was sitting, which marked the last resting place of Lord Wyatt of Weeford, the stone proclaiming that he was sadly missed by his wife Veruschka and his children Pericles and Petronella. Subsequent investigation confirmed my suspicion that, prior to his ennoblement, this had been Woodrow Wyatt, maverick MP and journalist, who also, obviously, had a fine and highly developed taste in Christian names.

I'd never been to Lichfield, didn't know a thing about the place and, to my recollection, had never had a conversation that even remotely touched upon the subject. And yet I liked it. Where had it been all my life? It had never written, never phoned.

I had a walk around the city centre and spent some time in the magnificent three-spired cathedral. I also had a chance to absorb some of the city's colourful Civil War history with the help of a couple of strategically positioned information plaques. My B&B was located in Lichfield's cathedral close (the second time on the walk that I'd had this priviledge – the first being Truro) and offered an excellent counterpoint to the rigours of the previous night at the pub in Kingsbury.

The only slight damper on an otherwise satisfactory situation was my choice of pub. I knew, even as I did it, that I was making a mistake, but sometimes you just can't help yourself. You've probably guessed, of course, that I was back in Wetherspoon territory again. Once more, Tim Martin had lavished generous care and attention on a pub, got plenty of nice beer in, and then forgotten that you also need someone to serve behind the bar. This was The Acorn, another barn of a place. It was a Thursday, so not the busiest night of the week. And yet by the time I finally managed to get served by the poor nine-year-old who could barely see over the top of the bar I was weeping with frustration.

My minor irritations were put into context by a conversation with my gracious and helpful hostess Jill Jones, a former gym teacher. She'd undergone no fewer than six hip operations. And there was me thinking that having to wait for my beer constituted a major problem.

I didn't feel too good the next morning, Friday 19 May. I think it was largely fatigue stemming from two consecutive broken nights' sleep. Staying in the cathedral close had been fine, but the downside was the constant intrusion of the cathedral bells into my slumbers. This was in wholesome contrast to the previous night when I'd tossed and turned for hours listening to the late night revelry at the pub in Kingsbury.

I breakfasted with George, an Australian manufacturer of children's costumes and party clothes, and John, a retired former executive with Debenhams. While I was merely rehearsing for retirement, John had pressed on to the real thing and was heavily engaged on the grandchildren front.

Initial progress that morning was dispiritingly slow. I had nothing booked by way of accommodation and was discovering by experience that, while on weeknights the B&B supply and demand equation normally favoured the buyer, the balance shifted at weekends and it wasn't always easy to find accommodation in the right place. I tried to phone as I walked across the fields out of Lichfield, using numbers assembled from a variety of sources, but this was Friday, many places were booked and the process was all very laborious and frustrating. I finally succeeded in securing beds for the next two nights, but my pace had been considerably reduced. I'd no sooner finished on the phone than it started to rain. Torrentially. It was one of those occasions (in retrospect mercifully rare) when teeth had to be gritted and each mile seemingly hacked out of granite.

At about 11 a.m. I arrived at a pub called The Drill Inn, just north of Burntwood. The place appeared closed but the lights were on, and I looked through the window more in hope than in expectation of any hospitality. It must have seemed like one of those allegorical illustrations from a Dickens novel – a ragged child in the cold and rain pressing its pathetic face to the window of a room with a blazing fire and vast quantities of food and drink laid out on a groaning table. And like many of the novels there was a happy ending here too, because I was spotted by a lady who was busily vacuuming the bar and invited inside. From this point the day improved out of all recognition. I was served a magnificent cup of coffee (proceeds waived in favour of the NSPCC) and was able to dry out and rest from the rigours of the morning. I swallowed a Mars bar, read the *Sun* and was treated to what I still think of as the apotheosis of the barmaid's cleavage. Its owner was classically blond and the cleavage itself was extremely deep, extremely tanned and was contained within a gratifyingly scanty white blouse. Taken as a whole, my visit to The Drill Inn was a deeply satisfying experience.

The rain stopped for a while and I gained elevation to the highest point of the Heart of England Way at the entrance to Cannock Chase. This was another part of England's geography of which I'd hitherto been entirely ignorant. I now know that the Chase is actually quite small – only 26 square miles in area – and rises very distinctly from the rolling green fields of Staffordshire. My walk on the Chase was brief, as I soon diverged from the path to descend on the road into Rugeley. This was an emotional moment, representing as it did my departure from the Heart of England Way and the end of a relationship that had lasted four-and-a-half companionable and largely harmonious days. The Way was now headed north-westwards and no longer served my purpose. In accordance with my philosophy of keeping the miles to a minimum, I needed to go due north and bring into play the next part of my route, namely the Staffordshire Way. Moving from one Way to the next involved a tricky piece of navigation through Rugeley, but after a sticky start to the day the force was now with me. I rendezvoused with the Staffordshire Way just north of Rugeley without difficulty and enjoyed the afternoon's walk in the sunshine past Blithfield Reservoir to Abbots Bromley.

Rugeley had appeared nondescript and Abbots Bromley also looked unremarkable, albeit in a much more pleasant and comfortable way. There was a cluster of old black-and-white cottages, a butter cross and a fine old parish church. The village is famous for its Horn Dance – an ancient ritual that makes cheese-rolling and shin-kicking appear hackneyed and mundane. The dance takes place in early September and involves a group of 12 men disporting themselves over a 10-mile course to various parts of the village. The happy band of 12 consists of a man on a hobby horse, a 'maid', a jester, a boy with bow and arrow, six men wearing reindeer antlers and two musicians on accordion and triangle. This bizarre ritual began in 1226 and nobody's got the faintest idea as to why it started or what it's for. Call me cynical but I reckon there's a fertility ritual in there somewhere.

If I remember right I had the choice of three pubs in Abbots Bromley that night. I went for the Goat's Head on the basis of its apparently superior food offering, and a wise choice this turned out to be. Strangely, for a Friday night, the place was virtually empty – worrying given that the food and beer were good and the service friendly and attentive. It made me wonder whether this was just another manifestation of the current travails of the British pub.

For although it's not an issue that has received wide media coverage, it's a regrettable fact that the British pub is in trouble. At present one pub closes its doors for good almost every single day and the problem is getting worse. Causes are variously ascribed to rising overheads, onerous regulation, changing social habits and a tendency for brewers to capitalize on their assets and sell their pubs to developers. There are, admittedly, a lot of bad pubs around, and it can be argued that a Darwinian process that weeds out the poorer places and forces others to improve isn't necessarily a bad thing. After all, many (most?) pubs have successfully reinvented themselves as honest, value-for-money restaurants. But I still can't help feeling uneasy about what the loss of a pub can mean to a community – especially in a rural area. I was encouraged to learn that my concern is shared by our august legislature, which has been sufficiently exercised by the problem to order an enquiry. The work has been entrusted to a worthy body called (and I'm not joking here) the All Party Parliamentary Beer Group. Given the nature of the Group's work, the inclusion of the words 'All Party' could perhaps be considered a tad ambiguous, but never mind. I await the conclusions of their report with interest. In the meantime the residents of Abbots Bromley should be mindful of the need to ensure that fine local amenities like The Goat's Head receive the support they deserve.

I'd covered 92 miles in the five days walking since Jane and I had gone our separate ways in Chipping Campden and that Friday, for the first time in three nights, I slept very soundly. One month had elapsed since the start of the walk, and I calculated the total distance covered from Land's End to Abbots Bromley was 427 miles. When talking about the walk, and my ultimate intention of reaching John O'Groats, I felt that these miles under the belt now gave me a modicum of credibility. When answering questions on the subject I didn't yet have quite the confidence in the final outcome to adopt the laconic Clint Eastwood style with accompanying steely glint in the eye. But I was getting there. Maybe by the time he reached Scotland the lone stranger strolling into town would have adopted the poncho, the cigarillo clenched between the teeth and full Enrico Morricone backing music.

Despite stepping on the gas and upping the daily average miles, the body was still responding. And crucially, despite fatigue and virtually continuous rain, the mind was in good shape too. I still felt eager to get on the road each morning. The programme for the next few days was a varied and interesting one. I now had the better part of two days on the Staffordshire Way before getting to Cheshire, the challenge of the Bollin Valley Way and Manchester Airport. This, as those asinine motorway signs around London say, would be *The North*. I also had another rest to look forward to. The next week end was the Spring Bank Holiday, which Jane and I planned to spend with her parents in Yorkshire, before she joined me again on the trail in another desperate attempt to raise standards of cuisine and hygiene. It all seemed exceptionally promising. All I had to do was to keep trudging.

7

In some respects the Staffordshire Way turned out to be something of a disappointment. This was partly because of the weather, which was unremittingly dire for the whole of the next two days. The rain undoubtedly hindered the Staffordshire Way in presenting itself to best advantage. It blocked out the views, muddied the fields and converted the approaches to stiles into water obstacles that closely resembled sheep dips.

There again the Staffordshire Way could have done more to show itself in a positive light. I'd invested in Staffordshire County Council's 'official guide' to the Way, which at first glance appeared to be a comprehensive and well-organized piece of work, but on closer examination (and of course my 'closer examination' only took place about four seconds prior to joining the Way at Rugeley) proved to be virtually useless for my purposes. The guides to the Cotswold Way and Heart of England Way had been skilfully arranged to assist walkers tackling the path in either direction. The producers of their Staffordshire counterpart, on the other hand, obviously believed that users of their path only walked from north to south. It clearly never occurred to them that some poor deluded soul might actually approach from the south and walk north. The text of the guide gave a very lucid description of the north–south course, but for awkward and contrary folk like me only the accompanying maps were of any potential value, and they added little or nothing to the information contained in my own Ordnance Survey maps. And before you ask – no, you can't read the text back to front, starting at the end and hoping it will lead you to the beginning. I tried and it just doesn't work. Nor does holding the text in front of a mirror.

Not only does the Staffordshire Way have an 'official guide' that is a complete waste of time for 50 per cent of its potential users, it has other more tangible defects. For one thing the waymarking is erratic in parts, so that, as I was to find to my cost, diverging from the trail is an ever-present possibility. And for another, I'd have to say that the stiles were not always conducive to the ease and comfort of an ageing hobo with a dodgy back carrying a 25-pound pack. I don't want to be too critical, because maintaining a trail requires a lot of effort, much of it supplied by volunteers, but having become something of an aficionado of the long-distance footpath, I'd have to conclude that the infra-structure of the Staffordshire Way suffers in comparison to that of the Cotswold and Heart of England trails.

Sorry about that, but the comments are a reflection of my surly and mutinous mood as I walked northwards to Uttoxeter on the morning of Saturday 20 May. I'd had a series of small mishaps, culminating in a heavy fall as I made a slippery and precarious descent to a waterlogged stile. No injuries were sustained, apart from a very muddy backside and badly wounded pride. By my count this was the fifth time I'd fallen over since Land's End. I also had a very lacklustre lunch at Colonel Mustard's Snack Bar in Uttoxeter, but the mood was soon lightened by a temporary improvement in the weather and, most notably, by a visit to the most spectacu-larly well-presented gentlemen's public convenience I've ever had the priviledge of using. It was tucked away unobtrusively at the northern end of Uttoxeter town centre and its exterior gave no hint of the wonders within. Not only was the place spotlessly clean and tidy but it was also bedecked with large, colourful bunches of flowers. A printed notice made it abundantly (possibly even aggressively) clear that the convenience was managed by a team of women. All I could do was salute the ladies involved in the creation of this masterpiece and retreat in awe.

I played truant from the Staffordshire Way that afternoon, taking the shorter route via lanes from Uttoxeter to Alton, rather than risking the circuitous and potentially more difficult course of the Way itself. From Alton, I followed the course of the abandoned North Staffordshire Railway along the valley of the River Churnet to Oakamoor. The rain restarted and grew steadily heavier. I'd never heard of the Churnet Valley but, even in these monsoon-like conditions it was a real gem. It's a narrow, steep-sided, abundantly wooded valley and, after all the rain of the previous few days, it was extravagantly lush and verdant. The cricket ground at Oakamoor was certainly lush and verdant as I paused to watch my first live cricket action of the season. It was a beautiful setting. The batsmen took guard after the tea interval and made a watchful start to their innings. The only discordant note was the pouring rain. It was getting heavier by the minute, but there was absolutely no sign of either umpires or players leaving the field or even displaying the slightest sign of discomfort at the steadily worsening conditions. Even though I was wearing full rain gear I snapped before the cricketers did; they were still playing as I turned and continued my walk into Oakamoor.

I stayed at the Beehive Guesthouse in Oakamoor, hosted by the excellent Colin and Ruth Franks. Excellent – but also very generous, because they donated the whole of my payment for bed and breakfast to the NSPCC. The spontaneous largesse of donors, most of them complete strangers, was humbling.

The scope of the opportunity for charitable fundraising

presented by a Land's End–John O'Groats walk became obvious even during the very early stages of planning. Not only is an end-to-end walk a relatively unusual event, it also lasts a very long time. Unlike other fundraising efforts, like fun-runs or concerts, the window of opportunity presented by LEJOG is open for weeks. As preparations progressed, the fundraising element absorbed substantial time and effort and, of course, with the help of props like Geoff's shirts I was also able to collect significant amounts of money en route.

I'd decided to walk on behalf of two causes. The first was the fund to finance repairs on the bells belonging to Phil the Vicar's church. My friend Bob, treasurer of the Parochial Church Council and also, coincidentally, Phil the Vicar's head bell ringer, sat down with me at our local over a couple of pints of Adnams one cold January night, and together we thrashed out our marketing strategy.

The response was gratifying, but while Bob's Bells was considered an excellent cause locally, it was never going to achieve seismic importance in a national context. The obvious choice for a parallel (and with due respect to Bob) more heavyweight cause was the NSPCC. It's something my wife and I have supported for a number of years. Jane is a district chairperson in Norwich and I just stand around on windy street corners rattling tins. And before anyone reading this gets the wrong idea I don't *really* rattle tins – at least not any more. My first outing as a NSPCC street collector one cold winter's day some years ago almost ended in disaster because I did, in all innocence, actually rattle my tin. In fact I did quite a bit more than just rattle. In my efforts to keep warm, and to stave off terminal boredom, I waved my arms and shouted at the passing shoppers like some latter day fairground hustler. My patter had the benefit of clarity and directness but it did, on reflection, lack subtlety and sophistication. It went something along the lines of 'Roll up, roll up – come on now – NSPCC – dig deep' and so on. The punters, especially the children, reacted very positively, and I had a steady stream of benefactors queuing to relieve themselves of their money. This went on for an hour or so in the middle of Norwich's main pedestrian shopping thoroughfare, at which point I was relieved from my post and returned happily to base with my collecting tin. Came the moment to count the proceeds and it was discovered to widespread astonishment that in the course of my one hour tour of duty I'd collected some £32 – an amount that compared very favourably with other tins which contained lesser amounts like £6.50 or £8.25. I was called upon to account for this apparent discrepancy and with a sense of quiet pride I explained the simple but obviously effective techniques that underpinned my success. It was only then, when the listening NSPCC officials (including my wife) began to turn ashen white, that I realized something might have gone badly wrong. In fact it was a moment rather akin to those cartoons by Bateman, which depict the horrified reaction to various crass but totally innocent gaffes: people faint, their hair stands on end, monocles fly out of eye sockets, etc. This cartoon (with apologies to Bateman) would have been entitled 'The Man who Rattled his Tin in Norwich City Centre'.

The point is, of course, that collectors are not permitted by law to make any promotional noise or gestures whatsoever. Even rattling the collecting tin is strictly forbidden. Any contravention of the regulations could lead to suspension from the streets and a ban on future collections. So I didn't rattle the tin on my walk, I let Geoff's shirts do the talking for me. But many people, like Mr and Mrs Franks, still showed immense generosity.

Oakamoor, like the Churnet Valley, was not flattered by the rain, but it was an attractive little place and I enjoyed my visit to The Lord Nelson. It was on my return from the pub that I was able to enjoy one of the few benefits of being alone on a Saturday night. If I'd been at home or in company I couldn't possibly have done what I did. Yes, I watched the *Eurovision Song Contest*. There – I've said it now. The truth's out. I've been a closet *Eurovision Song Contest* fan all my life. When you think about it, turning down party invitations, and telling people it's because you want to stay in and watch the *Eurovision Song Contest*, is probably unlikely to advance your social standing. And if you're at home with the family, asking to change channels so you can watch the show isn't a request that's going to endear you to teenage or early 20s offspring.

On this occasion, though, I was alone, and I made the most of this heaven-sent opportunity. However, I must firstly confess to an increasing sense of bafflement as to the eastern boundaries of Europe – at least when it comes to song contests or football competitions. For years now Europe seems to have included countries like Israel and Azerbaijan. Where will it all end? I have it on good authority that Iran and Saudi Arabia have applied to join UEFA and that next year's Eurovision Song Contest will be held in Rawalpindi.

Wherever it's held it will do well to better the 2006 edition. The winning entry came from Finland in the shape of a bizarre and most unprepossessing group of youths attired as Goths. Personally, I felt they had very little to recommend them. In my view they were comfortably outclassed by the lady from Macedonia with endless legs and frayed denim shorts, the blokes from Lithuania singing a song called 'We are the Winners' when they ever so patently weren't, and, best of all, a blond, tattooed Amazon from Turkey, clad in a tasseled mini–frock. As ever, Terry Wogan's commentary struck just the right sardonic note. The whole thing was priceless.

The next morning I rejoined the Staffordshire Way and walked north-westwards through the Hawksmoor Forest. The forest was pleasant but it didn't last more than a few minutes, and I was soon jolted back into the harsh normality

111

of the Staffordshire Way – a primitive stile followed by an absolute quagmire on the other side. What the Staffordshire Way must be like in winter, or after a really prolonged spell of wet weather, God only knows. But this quagmire was nothing compared to the one that confronted me a few minutes later. This was perhaps the perfect illustration of the way in which the walker can quickly move from a state of placid prosperity to one bordering on complete disaster in a few short seconds.

Firstly the grey skies broke and it started to rain. Heavily. I nevertheless opted to plough on – unwisely as it turned out because within seconds I was in the middle of the muddiest landscape I'd ever seen. It is no exaggeration to say that if it had been used as a backdrop for a film about the Battle of Passchendaele, or for one of those ritual humiliation Japanese game shows, it would have been considered ridiculously overdone. It was a broad uphill track hemmed in by woods, and the going was, to put it mildly, heavy. Every step forward was a minor triumph. The feeling soon started to dawn that this was bad even by Staffordshire Way standards and that maybe, just maybe, I'd departed from the correct route. I could see a gatepost in the distance with what looked like a waymark fixed to it so I struggled on up the hill.

I forget now what the waymark was for when I finally reached it, but it wasn't for the Staffordshire Way. So I was not only caught in the rain in the middle of Passchendaele but I was also lost. Things couldn't have been worse. Could they. Could they? Oh yes. Quite a lot worse really.

It's possible that the stress I was feeling was so palpable that it somehow communicated itself to inanimate objects, or maybe there was some malign force field operating in the area. Whatever the reason, it was at that precise moment that the left lens of my spectacles decided to eject itself spontaneously from its frame and describe a graceful parabola as it fell into the mud. My sight, already severely limited by the misting effects of exertion, was now reduced even further. And the surface of the ground was so viscous and liquefied that the point of impact of the lens was already difficult to make out.

Older readers will remember those Hamlet cigar ads depicting moments when things take a turn for the worse. I could almost hear the music from the ads as I stood by the gatepost. But as the strains of Bach's 'Air on a G String' trickled through my mind I realized that there was a further, even bleaker, dimension to all this. My mind went back to the moment in Balsall Street when my best pair of spectacles had disintegrated in my hands. What now lay in the mud was the lens out of my *spare* pair of glasses.

The series of setbacks had been so rapid that I stood there in a state of semi-shock waiting for some further calamity to occur. As I did so, the brain was involuntarily performing a number of calculations. It was Sunday. No opticians open today. The nearest one maybe not until Macclesfield where I hoped to arrive Monday lunchtime. How to cope with acute myopia in the mean time? Charter a guide dog? Find a white stick? Oh dear. I was in deep sh*t both literally and metaphorically.

On balance, it was crucial that I find the lens. I took off my rucksack, knelt squinting in the mud with my face inches from the surface and, mercifully, was able to locate it without too much difficulty. I then had to wipe it and try to get it back into its frame. I'll draw a discreet veil over the accompanying language but I managed this feat as well, which in retrospect is quite surprising. When you're in a hole, rule number one says you stop digging. So, next, I reversed course back downhill into Passchendaele, hoping to re-locate the Staffordshire Way. If anything, the downhill was even worse than going up. I found that keeping my feet demanded huge reserves of concentration and physical dexterity that I didn't know I possessed. But the incentive for staying upright was huge. If I *had* fallen over in that mud it would have been extremely difficult to get upright again and God alone knows what I would have looked like when I'd finished.

By some fluke, towards the bottom of the hill I saw it – a waymark for the Staffordshire Way placed at an angle to the path that made it visible only to a dwarf and, to boot, only to one with eyes sharpened by a lifelong diet of carrot juice. By contrast I'm 6 feet 2 inches tall and short-sighted, so the chances of anyone like me spotting this signpost were just about zero. The signpost marked a point where, for reasons known only to itself, the Staffordshire Way abandoned a broad straight track in favour of turning sharply along a narrow, inconsequential-looking path beside a wall. It really should have been better signposted. I wondered how many other innocent walkers had been lured to a muddy doom.

All this had cost me an inordinate amount of time, and the conditions ensured that progress continued to be slow. I paused at the store in Kingsley Holt to buy a newspaper and some supplies, and I don't think I have ever been greeted with less enthusiasm by a shopkeeper than by the lady behind the counter. She was definitely not impressed by the steaming hulk that was depositing copious quantities of rainwater on to her clean floor.

When I exited the shop, uttering abject apologies, the Staffordshire Way immediately contrived to get me lost once again in what was, after all, only a small village. I tried to rectify the situation by asking directions from a kindly old gentleman I met in the churchyard, but the conversation had to be abandoned because of the man's Alsatian dog, whose obvious sole ambition in life was to rip my throat out. The animal was on its hind legs barking and snarling with saliva dripping from its jaws. I departed the scene before the Alsatian's brute force became too much for the old gentleman's shaky grip on the leash. The morning was not going well.

114

But it did get better. I found my way through Kingsley, and towards lunchtime descended a steep path back down into the Churnet Valley. The view over the valley as I did so was composed entirely of shades of grey – the low cloud and drizzle combining with mist and blasts of steam from a distant railway locomotive whose echoing whistle provided an excellent final touch of atmosphere. 'Paint that one, Turner', I thought.

The improvement in my fortunes was maintained as I joined another canal, which shared the valley with the river and a railway. It was the Caldon Canal, completed in 1779 and one of the first major canal restoration projects in the UK. Renovation work lasted between 1970 and 1974. The railway was the Churnet Valley Railway, which operates from Leekbrook southwards to Oakamoor, and is a surviving part of the former North Staffordshire Railway from North Rode, near Macclesfield, to Uttoxeter. Canal and railway share the valley as far as Cheddleton, where I finally managed to swallow some lunch huddled under a bridge to escape the rain. There was compensation for my various tribulations in a sighting of the 2-6-4 tank engine that I had heard back at Kingsley.

On a better day the afternoon's walk would have been very scenic. Even in the rain the walk along the canal and, subsequently, alongside Rudyard Reservoir wasn't at all bad. I found out that many years ago the reservoir had been a favourite haunt of a certain Mr and Mrs Kipling, a discovery that cleared up another of life's little mysteries.

After Rudyard the rain finally stopped and the Staffordshire Way gave me one final valedictory bonus by slipping in another mile of railway in the evening sunshine. It was the North Staffordshire Railway again – this section, like the first I'd walked south of Oakamoor the previous day, was now abandoned. I particularly enjoyed the name of a pub I passed on the railway at Rushton Spencer. 'The Knot Inn' must

115

have caused the odd piece of confusion in conversations over the years.

After Rushton Spencer the Staffordshire Way turns west and then south-west to its final resting place at Mow Cop near Congleton. Its usefulness to me had therefore expired, and I left it, turning north along the lanes below the enigmatically named hill known as 'The Cloud'. The Staffordshire Way had not given me the steady, reliable support which the Cotswold Way and Heart of England Way had provided over the last two weeks. Ours had been a difficult and sometimes tempestuous relationship. But it's often the stormy, demanding, love–hate relationships that are the most memorable.

I arrived at my night's resting place at Bosley at about 6.45p.m., having left Oakamoor some ten hours previously. I'd covered over 20 miles and it had been a long and difficult day. But it wasn't over yet. I was learning from experience that a Sunday evening wasn't always the easiest time to find food. Bosley had one restaurant (closed) and two pubs. I hurried down to the Harrington Arms. No food. With a sense of dire foreboding I crossed the road to the Queen's Arms. I could tell immediately that I was too late here as well because the staff were taking a well-earned rest on the customers' side of the bar.

Fortunately, the staff were women (I really don't think my tactics would have stood the remotest chance of working if they'd been blokes). All I could do was give them the big old sob story – the rain, Passchendaele, getting lost – and throw myself on their mercy. I'd already come across a number of heroines on the walk, and at the Queen's Arms in Bosley another one emerged to take her place on the podium. Her name was Janet, and even after an ever-lengthening interval of time, her act of charity still makes me quite dewy-eyed in reminiscence. Having served me a pint of Boddingtons cask bitter, she retired to the kitchen and emerged with the biggest plate of cheese sandwiches I'd ever seen. It was immense. And it was exactly what was required.

I enjoyed a very convivial time at the Queen's Arms and also relished drinking the Boddingtons again. It was the staple beer of my youth. Memory fades and perceptions change, but in the many intervening years I think it has lost that acrid, real bitter taste – or maybe it's just that my palate has lost its youthful edge. Irrespective of this minor quibble, Janet, the Queen's Arms and the Boddingtons provided a splendid finale to the day.

Bosley had been memorable for the first signpost showing the magic word 'Manchester'. This was definitely 'The North'. The regional TV news programme on the morning of Monday 22 May had been 'North West' news. At Macclesfield I took the opportunity of updating the blog, and there is a strong undertone of barely suppressed excitement in the unusually effusive first sentence. I wrote 'It's a wet Monday in Macclesfield. But this is Cheshire – and in my book that's the North of England. Manchester is only 18 miles away and the accents reflect the fact.' I was, after all, coming home.

The gentle trudge along the Macclesfield Canal from Bosley that morning had been pleasant and, above all, dry. But the weather forecast was, once again, appalling, and the gentle trudge got me into Macclesfield only just ahead of the advancing rain. I put on the familiar rain gear under a handy bus shelter. I'm afraid I can't resist mentioning that the Macclesfield Canal has the distinction of being surveyed by Thomas Telford and, in its upper section, of being the second highest navigable waterway in the land after The Huddersfield Narrow Canal. Sorry about that. Just thought you might be interested.

I lunched in Macclesfield bus station, reflecting on the fact that the lunch venues had again slipped into their familiar mediocre rut. There was no way that Jane was going to put up with the likes of this when she joined the trail in a few

117

days. Colonel Mustard's Café in Uttoxeter and the canal bridge in Cheddleton wouldn't have impressed her much either.

I would have liked to linger in Macclesfield – the Silk Museum in particular looked like a good piece of northern industrial heritage and well worth a visit. But I was approaching the pivot of the whole Land's End–John O'Groats walk, the crux of the entire project. This was, of course, the Bollin Valley Way – the carefully selected cornerstone of the complex, interconnecting set of trails designed to get me to Lancashire, the canals and beyond. If the Bollin Valley Way didn't work as advertised, if there wasn't, after all, this fabled tunnel under Manchester Airport, I might, despite all my planning, have to resort to the Pennine Way. And that, after all that I'd endured, would be a fate that was just too horrendous to contemplate.

I was too keyed up to linger at the Silk Museum. So I left Macclesfield in heavy rain and a mild state of trepidation. But it was there OK – in exactly the spot indicated in a colourful, if rather minimalist, set of brochures kindly sent to me by Cheshire County Council. The Bollin Valley Way even has its own waymark, a racy little blue and green number, that appeared with gratifying frequency as I walked out of town parallel with (believe it or not) the River Bollin and the railway line to Stockport and Manchester. The frequency of waymarks soon diminished and seemed to give out altogether as I neared Wilmslow. I lost the trail eventually but was close enough to Wilmslow for it not to matter. Once again, in decent weather this would have been a pleasant afternoon's walk but the incessant rain somewhat marred the enjoyment. The little River Bollin had been transformed into a raging torrent and at one point had swept the path away, thereby enforcing a detour on to a nearby road.

Wilmslow lies on the southern edge of Manchester. There aren't many up-market addresses in Manchester but

Wilmslow is one of them. Growing up in Manchester, I didn't have much call to go to Wilmslow, but my recollection is of a place with a villagey, rural feel. In the intervening time, though, it's had its heart ripped out. The town is now bisected by a four-lane highway that sits at the bottom of what looks like a concrete canyon: I didn't take to the place at all.

My jaundiced view of Wilmslow was heavily influenced by the fact that it won the booby prize for the worst B&B of the entire walk. It was not only the worst – it was the worst by a very considerable margin. In fact, on reflection, it was the *only* bad one – but, boy, was it bad.

It all got off on the wrong foot when I drove a hard bargain with the landlady. Jennifer (not her real name) quoted me an exceedingly ambitious £39 for bed and breakfast. I'd not started these negotiations until my arrival in Macclesfield, so while my counter-offer of £30 may have looked unattractive, it was probably the best offer Jennifer was going to get in the limited time available. To add insult to injury I'd conducted the transaction through the intermediary of the Tourist Information Office in Macclesfield who, quite naturally, charge a small commission for their services – a further deduction of £3 from Jennifer's fee.

As luck would have it, only very shortly after closing the deal with me, Jennifer had apparently received an enquiry from a less parsimonious punter who was quite happy to pay the full £39. So Jennifer was some £12 out of pocket, but that was absolutely no excuse for the miserable, carping reception she extended to a wet and very weary traveller. It wasn't as if her place was the Ritz either. There was no en-suite and the accommodation was cramped and tired. But the epic centrepiece of Jennifer's hospitality-free zone was the breakfast. Jennifer had pioneered an entirely new concept in guest management – a beacon for the British tourist industry to follow.

119

It was the takeaway breakfast.

I stood slack-jawed with amazement as Jennifer explained how it worked. The 'breakfast', which consisted of a packet of cornflakes, a carton of orange juice and a granola bar, all of minuscule proportions, could, in theory, be eaten on the spot but Jennifer's clear preference was for the guest to vacate the premises and go elsewhere before sitting down to consume this sumptuous feast. I commented politely that this was the first time I'd come across this arrangement since Land's End and that I found it a tad unusual. Quite unfazed, Jennifer explained that many of her guests were young men who spent the night carousing and were consequently unable to appreciate the splendours of a full English breakfast. I confessed to being quite sympathetic to the general concept of carousing but stressed to Jennifer that it rarely detracted from my enjoyment of a hearty breakfast. Despite my eloquence she remained completely unmoved. It was the take-away breakfast or nothing.

Reflecting on the conversation and on Jennifer's carousing guests rationale, I decided that she probably got the guests she deserved. I subsequently looked through the visitors' book to check for any expressions of grateful thanks or glowing praise, but the comments of previous visitors had been neutral and terse. I wish I'd had the courage to write something like 'This poxy place represents the worst value for money since Land's End'.

But I didn't. In fact I made a final effort to ingratiate myself with Jennifer. Returning later that evening from the King William (Robinsons bitter – good stuff), I was surprised to find her outside in the drizzle and gathering gloom. She was using some kind of pressure-hose apparatus in an attempt to remove the moss and slime from the plastic roof of the miserable car-port arrangement at the side of the house. She clearly needed help, and I did my level best to obey her shouted instructions to turn taps on or off before the encroaching dusk and rain finally drove us inside. I thought this gallant action went way above and beyond the call of duty for a house guest, but it still wasn't enough to persuade Jennifer to upgrade my breakfast.

The next day was Tuesday 23 May and the sun was shining – which was a giant leap for mankind despite my sketchy breakfast. It had rained virtually non-stop for the past three days and for a large slice of the time since I'd left Chipping Campden. But the weather was changing and it was to be a while before I saw rain again.

The Bollin Valley Way had long since lost its initial enthusiasm for waymarks and I got lost for 15 minutes or so not long after leaving Wilmslow. However, I recovered the trail and moved on north-westwards. I could soon hear the whine of jet engines and, as I walked, the noise got closer. This was the day for walking underneath Manchester Airport. My guide to the Bollin Valley Way was quite categoric it was going to happen and I had no reason to disbelieve it. It was just that if, for some reason, the tunnel turned out to be inoperative or closed, the consequences were dire. I'd somehow have to walk around Manchester Airport, which, as detours go, would be pretty demanding. Any recourse to motorized transport to get out of this predicament was naturally against the rules of the end-to-end walk.

As the noise of aero engines grew steadily louder I encountered one of the (by now quite infrequent) Bollin Valley Way waymarks. Affixed to it was a notice saying 'Boggy Ground' followed by a telephone number. This was clearly some kind of boggy ground helpline. The notice also gave a name – the clear inference being that a certain Malcolm Ainsworth was on hand, poised eagerly by the phone, to field any boggy ground questions that might arise. I wrote the number down. If the Bollin Valley Way supremos thought it necessary to provide a boggy ground helpline, then the degree of ground bogginess must be inordinately severe – probably far exceeding that which I'd encountered during the Passchendaele episode in Staffordshire. I carried on, thinking that in the space of a morning I'd gone from one extreme to another – from one regime where customer care was a completely unknown concept to one where, thanks to Malcolm, the customer was king. Given the current way of the world, I strongly suspected that if things went badly awry I'd be offered 'counselling' as well. I was most impressed.

In the end Malcolm's help wasn't required. The path rejoined my old friend the River Bollin and I was instantly rewarded with a first sighting of an aircraft. It was a Singapore Airlines 747, quite close, climbing away to my left. And then, very soon afterwards, there it was – a cavernous hole in the embankment which supported the runway. The path became a gravel track which ran alongside the river into the tunnel. It was a long tunnel, too, although its height ensured there was more than sufficient natural light. And then I was through and the roar of the planes was coming from behind me.

The Bollin Valley Way, God bless it, continues westwards to Warburton, where there is a road bridge over the Manchester Ship Canal, and then on to the petrochemical town of Partington. Although it had done me proud, and in spite of the great sense of comfort and security I derived from having Malcolm's helpline to fall back on, I decided, especially in view of the wet ground conditions, that I could reach Warburton more quickly by an alternative route. So I bade farewell to the Bollin near a small place called Thorns Green and continued up into Hale at the extreme south-western corner of the Manchester conurbation. Suburban Manchester is not the normal setting for rucksacks, walking boots and people with map cases slung round their necks, and I attracted a few curious glances as I progressed up the main street. Of course I'd walked through all kinds of urban environments during the last few weeks, but this was the first time that I'd been engaged in banter and repartee with fellow pedestrians. Your average Mancunian is extremely warm and hospitable but, he also tends to be slightly brash and inquisitive and likes to let you know he's there. So various comments were thrown in my direction; there was a suggestion that I should get myself a sat-nav system and someone else enquired if I was a part of an expedition to trace the source of the A538. It was unsolicited but entirely humorous and benevolent – all in that flat and frankly rather dopey Manchester accent. Welcome home, Steve. I hope I gave as good as I got.

As I was home, I thought it was appropriate that I walked straight into industrial heritage. From Altrincham I covered a short stretch of the Bridgewater Canal. This was Britain's first canal, built in the 1760s by the Duke of Bridgewater to transport his coal into Manchester from Worsley, a few miles north-west of the city. It was a ground-breaking development. It was also my 'home' canal. I'd grown up about two miles away. The Duke had gone on to construct an extension to Runcorn and it was this that was now taking me westwards away from the city.

However, I very quickly switched from canal to rail – the bed of the disused line between Warrington and Broadheath which closed in 1985 and is now part of the Trans Pennine Trail. I passed the old station house at Dunham Massey, which was apparently a regular winner of the regional best-kept station award. This was no doubt because it was under female management. The information board showed a lovely photograph of Mrs Armstrong and Mrs Pat Bonnell, who was the last station mistress, displaying a formidable array of certificates from British Railways London Midland Region for 'best-kept station gardens and cleanliness and tidiness'. My mind went back to the wonderful public convenience in Uttoxeter.

It was straight, it was flat, the sun shone and I'd just come under Manchester Airport. In an hour or so I'd get to the Ship Canal. I'd just been passed by a very attractive blonde lady on a white horse and had, as a consequence, given voice to an excellent Leslie Phillips impression. And then, just for old times' sake, the railway crossed my little old mate the Bollin again. It was another of those moments when the endorphins flooded into the bloodstream and I felt very content.

I must confess to feeling a sense of real achievement as I walked through the village of Warburton and up to the bridge over the Ship Canal. From Chipping Campden I'd covered 158 miles in nine days through weather that had been largely atrocious on a route that had ingeniously threaded together four separate long-distance footpaths. As I crested the rise and got my first glimpse of the Canal it was a moment akin to Peter O'Toole and Omar Sharif arriving at the top of that sand dune overlooking Aqaba, or Livingstone at Lake Tanganyika. I paused and relished the scene then turned round and caught the bus back into Altrincham.

I was back at the Canal early the next morning courtesy of Mike. I'd stayed with him and his wife Ann overnight in Timperley and he'd very kindly offered to drive me back to the Canal rather than leave me to heave the rucksack on and off the bus. Mike and Ann are old friends from university days and, while we'd stayed in touch, the last time we'd enjoyed their hospitality we'd all been festooned with babies and young children. I caught up with one of the young children now – Alastair, geography graduate, IT professional and friend of Andrew 'Freddie' Flintoff. The other 'baby', Lucy, was away at university. Although Ann was still working, Mike had retired and was able to focus on important things like bird watching, sailing and walking. It was good to catch up with them again.

The Ship Canal is 112 years old but the sheer scale and vision of the thing still astounds me. To call it a canal is slightly misleading. These weren't barges or pleasure cruisers that had, in years gone by, travelled into the centre of Manchester, but ocean-going cargo ships of 10,000 tons or more. It was surreal to watch these monsters gliding silently across the fields of South Lancashire. In places you could see them for miles across the flat landscape.

I guess I'm more than slightly biased in my assessment but, as a Mancunian, I can't help feeling a certain pride, as well as admiration for the Manchester businessmen who had the vision and effrontery to conceive of a channel big enough to bring ocean-going ships 36 miles inland and turn a land-locked city into the nation's fourth largest port. And much of the vision, of course, sprang from the Mancunian's age-old mistrust of the Scouser. Liverpool was a perfectly serviceable deep-water port, but for decades there had been concern in Mancunian business circles about the high rates it was charging. The worldwide economic depression of the 1870s brought matters to a head, as Manchester gradually lost its competitive edge. There was an obvious need to reduce the overall cost of the city's exports – it was famously calculated that it cost more to send goods from Manchester to Liverpool than from London to Bombay. Firstly, there were dock charges to consider and the scousers demanded an additional levy for all goods passing through their port. Manchester's civic leaders also believed that most of the money raised was not spent on the dock facilities but on improving the wider city of Liverpool. It was akin to asking Manchester United supporters to pay for the re-construction of Anfield.

Ted Gray's excellent book on the Canal records that 'on the 27 June 1882 the historic meeting, which proved to be the first formal step in the Ship Canal project, took place at the Didsbury home of Daniel Adamson'. The meeting decided to set up a Provisional Committee and passed a finely crafted resolution, which was full of long words, but whose basic thrust was 'Bugger this for a game of soldiers – let's build a canal'.

Which, of course, they eventually did. It was by some distance the largest civil engineering project ever undertaken in Britain. Construction took six years and cost £15 million. What it would cost today is anybody's guess. It wasn't just the 36-mile-long channel – there were bridges, locks, sluices and harbours, not to mention some ten miles of embankments and sea walls where the Canal ran alongside the tideway and foreshore between Eastham and Runcorn.

As a very young Manchester schoolboy one of my favourite excursions was the short bus ride to Barton to see the two swing bridges over the canal. One bridge carried the road and the other was the aqueduct which carried the Bridgewater Canal. The latter was designed as a kind of sealed trough to be swung while full of water. Both bridges had to swing to allow boats on the Ship Canal to pass. In the mid-1960s a new, much higher, bridge was built which provided an uninterrupted road crossing over the Canal, so two generations of Mancunians have now grown up without knowing what it feels like to be 'bridged' – i.e. to have your road journey brought to a grinding (and potentially quite lengthy) halt at Barton Bridge. Our part of the city was served by a maternity hospital on the other side of the Canal, and that journey via Barton must have been a tense affair for expectant mothers in the days before the new bridge. My mother did it twice.

The bridge at Warburton is a toll bridge. Motorists are charged the princely sum of 12p to cross, but my coins were politely declined by the custodian in his box. The fee is waived for pedestrians. I crossed the bridge.

I could glimpse the outlying western fingers of the Pennines and gave thanks once again that I wasn't up there on Black Bog Pike, or wherever, but down here. I could now walk the next 70 miles or so on the flat and in a more or less straight line. The cunning plan was working. I walked up to Leigh along a short local footpath called the Glazebrook Trail

126

(sponsored by Timberland). I'd already done the Ship Canal, but the Glazebrook Trail took me across two more of the end-to-end walk's great natural barriers – the M62 and the East Lancs Road. That only left Hadrian's Wall and I'd be home and dry.

It was a bright but cold and windy day and there were breakers on Leigh Flash. The Flash is a large lake formed over 100 years ago by mining subsidence, and it is now, in the modern idiom, a 'country park'. It forms part of a corridor of wetland sites that run along the track of the Leeds–Liverpool canal between Leigh and Wigan. I passed Ince Moss, another of these flashes, later that same afternoon. Here again mining subsidence had created the flash – Ince Moss pit closed in 1962. It's encouraging to see nature healing over Lancashire's old industrial scars. Mike had talked with great enthusiasm about another flash near Warrington that was home to a colony of the extremely rare black-necked grebe. According to the Wildlife Trust for Lancashire, Manchester and North Merseyside, the flashes around Wigan host over 200 species of bird, 15 species of dragonfly and six types of orchid. Interestingly, the remaining colliery spoil and ash provides excellent conditions for a wide variety of wild flowers including, apparently, such rare species as round-leaved wintergreen, marsh helleborine and yellow bird's nest.

Nature's reclamation of the old industrial heartland was fine, but as I walked along the Leeds Liverpool Canal that afternoon I wondered what this meant for Wigan and its inhabitants. No more coal, no more cotton – and you don't make a living from black-necked grebes or round-leaved wintergreen. I hadn't been to Wigan for 40 years – so I was keen to have a look at the place.

Entering Wigan on the canal brings you straight to Wigan Pier. The pier, of course, was not a pier but an old shed with a small wharf at the side of the canal. It's now been converted into a museum with associated gift shop and snack bar as well as a pub called, perhaps unsurprisingly, The Orwell. The museum was just closing as I arrived, so this particular line of enquiry was blocked. Across the road was Trencherfield Mill, a classic, massive old mill building, also closed, and now, as far as I could gather, like the pier, a part of the tourist attraction called the Wigan Pier Experience. I walked up into the town.

The main street contains two railway stations and I was staying in the enigmatically named Swan and Railway Hotel right next to Wigan North Western, the larger of the two. The Railway part was pretty clear – quite where the Swan came from was less obvious. At £25 for bed and breakfast I couldn't have legitimately expected hotel accommodation that was anything better than spartan. But this was OK – neat, clean and, on the walls, some excellent old action photographs of Wigan Rugby League heroes. Its central location also gave me the chance to have a good look at the centre of Wigan.

It's impossible in one evening to arrive at any reasoned conclusions about a town and how it's doing, but there were clues. Paul Theroux devotes several pages to Wigan in his excellent *The Kingdom by The Sea*, published in 1983. This was the high tide of Thatcherism and a time, if you're old enough to recall it, when the traditional industries of the North of England were being decimated. There were swathes of job losses every week without the slightest compensating creation of new ones. It was a desperate time. Any generation of fresh employment opportunities was greeted with huge relief. If a newsagent took on a couple of new paperboys it was cause for wild celebration. Paul Theroux wrote of the high unemployment in Wigan and of 'deadly calm – which was also like panic – and an overwhelming emptiness'. The Wigan that George Orwell had described had been a place of squalor and suffering, but while Orwell had had a stab at envisaging 1984, there was no way he could have foreseen

1983. Theroux wrote 'What Orwell had not reckoned on – no one had – was that the bottom would fall out, and that in this post-industrial slump, with little hope of recovery, Wigan would be as bereft of energy and as empty a ruin as Stonehenge.'

Well Wigan had certainly progressed since 1983. It had clearly moved on a little even by 1995 when it received a visit from another great American travel writer, Bill Bryson. It's not clear how much time Bryson spent in Wigan but it obviously wasn't long. In *Notes From a Small Island* he contented himself with a few observations on 'the handsome and well maintained town centre' and the shops which seemed 'prosperous and busy' and then took the train to Liverpool where 'they were having a festival of litter when I arrived'.

The Wigan of 2006 had clearly made a good recovery. The Galleries shopping centre and the Market Place *are* handsome, and the main street was no more or less prosperous looking than any other town I'd passed through. It stood up pretty well against the likes of Uttoxeter, Rugeley or Wellington.

I'd have to counterbalance this slightly by saying that there were a few other less promising, but nonetheless tell-tale indications of the town's economic standing. Firstly there was nobody, absolutely nobody, around. OK, it was only Wednesday, but I would have expected a bit more life on the streets.

And I couldn't find anywhere to eat. For some bizarre reason I'd developed a craving, probably akin to those that suddenly and unaccountably overtake pregnant women. This craving was for a curry. I realized that a curry with associated trimmings and a couple of pints of lager would comfortably exceed the daily budget, but I just had to have one. It was an utterly desperate craving and it just had to be assuaged, whatever the cost. There were plenty of takeaway places, but

I didn't want a takeaway – I wanted a clean tablecloth, a tall glass of Cobra and a decent vindaloo. I walked all round the deserted centre of Wigan and couldn't find a curry house. And there weren't any other kinds of restaurant either. *All* the eateries were of the takeaway variety. In my experience a place without restaurants is a place where there's not a great deal of cash left over at the end of the week.

And in common with other demonstrably less wealthy places in South Lancashire, some of the people looked stunted and poorly. There seemed to be a much higher proportion of folk who were clearly not well, or supported by sticks, or driving around on those electric buggy contraptions.

I guess on balance that, while Wigan has done well, and the grebes and the wintergreen can be accounted as good things, much money flows into Wigan that is essentially generated elsewhere. Taxes paid in more prosperous places have gone to underpin the development of Wigan's infrastructure and the support of its citizens.

I missed out on the curry eventually. I was driven in desperation to the one place in the town centre where one could actually sit down with a knife and fork of an evening. Full marks to J.D. Wetherspoon for providing what was tantamount to a social service. The Moon Under Water dispensed an excellent pint of Moorhouse's Pride of Pendle bitter.

As a footnote, it was in Wigan that I finally evolved the technique of dealing with the difficulties that Wetherspoon puts in the way of its customers by refusing to man its pubs properly. When I *eventually* managed to get served I ordered my entire night's consumption of food and drink in one fell swoop. There's a danger of the beer going slightly flat but it's better than risking terminal apoplexy while you're waiting at the bar for refills.

I was away early the next morning. I had to be. I was aiming for Preston and the route along the Leeds Liverpool Canal, and then along suburban roads, was an eye-watering

26 miles, the longest day's walk of the trip so far. It was Thursday 25 May and I had the comfort of being able to look forward to the bank holiday weekend ahead to recover from the day's exertions.

There was an early reminder of Wigan's lost industrial infrastructure as I walked past swathes of vacant territory on the route north-west out of the town. The only building of any note in this post-industrial wasteland was the silver-grey meccano structure that is the JJB football stadium, home of Wigan Athletic. Its out of town location and its futuristic architecture symbolized the huge changes to football following the disasters of Heysel and Hillsborough. It occurred to me that Wigan was the first town I'd come through that boasted a league football club.

I spent most of the day on the Liverpool Leeds Canal – through Appleby Bridge and Parbold and then turning due north on the Rufford Branch which links the main canal to the Ribble estuary. As canals go it's a cracker. One of the great arteries of the industrial revolution, it's 127 miles long, rises 487 feet as it crosses the Pennines and achieves this feat with the help of 92 locks. It certainly made for rapid progress, the only problem being the onset of mild boredom at the unchanging nature of the scenery.

Lunch at Rufford church was enlivened by a conversation with some affable guys who were doing some restoration work in the graveyard. We tried out our forensic skills by attempting to identify some old bones they'd come across in the course of their labours, but the pieces had degenerated to such an extent it was impossible to tell from which part of the body they'd originated.

I left the canal some way north of Rufford and followed a direct course through Much Hoole, Walmer Bridge, Longton and the suburbs of Preston itself. The entry into Preston from the south over the Ribble is impressive. And in Preston I had absolutely no difficulty whatsoever in finding a curry.

Preston was half-time on the walk. I'd covered 535 miles since Land's End. I felt fit and confident that, barring accidents, I could now finish this thing. There'd been a few minor physical improvements – I'd lost a few pounds and had acquired a tan. But I'd also noticed a distinct behavioural change. To my surprise I was becoming increasingly prone to unexpected and uncharacteristic flashes of patience.

I noticed this particularly when I shopped. The stores where I stopped to buy supplies were often the small village post office-cum-general store type of establishment. My previous persona would have avoided these places like the plague because I knew, just knew, that before I could execute my blindingly simple four-second transaction I'd have to wait in line while five successive old ladies each had dealings with the shopkeeper that could only be measured in geological time. For each the conversation was probably the social event of the week, and the agenda would be long and complex. It would begin with a comprehensive review of the old lady's impressive range of minor ailments, progress to a detailed analysis of her dietary requirements and the impact these had on her shopping list, take in a few random detours through such rich and fertile conversational territory as the weather and last week's flower show before finally, finally getting within range of the actual commercial transaction itself. There'd then be a further lengthy hiatus because the lady had forgotten her purse or remembered another extraneous item that hadn't appeared on her original shopping list. Meanwhile my former pre-walk persona would be standing there with veins pulsing visibly and dangerously in its forehead, quite clearly on the cusp of a massive cardiac arrest.

Now, though, the shiny new LEJOG persona would smile tolerantly at these antics, would rejoice that in a busy, modern world there were still places where these homely goings-on and old-time courtesies still flourished, and it might even politely surrender its place in the queue to let a sixth old lady begin another summit conference with the shopkeeper. In Wilmslow my shiny new LEJOG persona had meekly accepted the takeaway breakfast scenario with a smile and a shrug, but its predecessor would almost certainly have adopted an entirely different tack. The result would have been either (a) the presentation by Jennifer of a full English breakfast complete with fresh flowers and an ironed copy of *The Times* or (b) a patchy night's sleep for the pre-walk persona on a convenient park bench.

I was warming to this new persona, although I was sceptical of its ability to survive when it returned to the real world. And of course, for all its virtues and new-found patience, there was still no way it could cope with J.D. Wetherspoon pubs.

But a return to the real world – at least for a couple of days – was what now awaited me. It was time to take a break. It was pouring with rain on the morning of Friday 26 May. I went to the library in Preston, did a few chores, admired the wonderful Victorian town hall and then walked about a mile and a half to the edge of town as far as the Lancaster Canal. I could resume from this point with Jane and not need to trouble her with the urban bit.

Job done. I turned round, walked back into Preston and took the train to meet Jane in Yorkshire.

8

You may have read Proust, but even if you haven't, you probably understand the concept of a Proustian moment. Proust has one of his characters bite into a cake and then blathers on for pages about how the taste suddenly triggers all kinds of memories that have been buried for years in the subconscious. I had my own Proustian moment on the Lancaster Canal on bank holiday Monday afternoon. As Jane and I walked past a small cabin cruiser tethered to the bank, the silence was pierced by the unmistakeable tones of the young Michael Caine in one of his formative roles as Lieutenant Bromhead. Yes, it was the 927th repeat on British TV of the classic film *Zulu*, currently holding in thrall the boat's crew, a solitary middle-aged male, clutching a can of beer and watching intently. For me, bank holiday Mondays and *Zulu* are inextricably intertwined, and Caine's voice evoked the memory of many a long-buried lazy afternoon. If I hadn't been out doing my walk I would have been at home watching. Great film, *Zulu*. One of these days I might actually get the hang of the plot. (Only joking.)

We'd left Preston at about 2 p.m. and walked up the canal for about 11 miles as far as the village of Bilsborrow. It was undemanding stuff and despite Jane's problems in the Cotswolds I had high hopes that we'd be able to capitalize on the flat terrain and cover 18 miles to Lancaster the following day. Once again Jane looked like something out of a fashion catalogue. With the sun behind us I compared our respective shadows as we walked – the one neat, trim and shapely, and the other strangely irregular, with odd-looking shapes straggling from the rucksack. These were a variety of straps and buckles whose function I still hadn't worked out, even after more than 500 miles on the road.

Jane and I had spent the weekend with her parents in Yorkshire. To say I'd enjoyed the rest would be an understatement. My mother-in-law had treated me like a conquering hero and I'd been cosseted to within an inch of my life. I was also able to catch up belatedly with the progress of the cricket season. It seems rather tame to label my father-in-law as a cricket enthusiast. Let's just say that when he got married I'm sure his first thought when he entered the church was to wonder whether the nave would take spin.

After weeks of walking, any journey in a wheeled conveyance was a real treat, and the train ride over the Pennines that morning had been no exception. The journey from Leeds to Preston is one of the most interesting and scenic in these islands. It passes through Halifax, Hebden Bridge, Burnley, Accrington and Blackburn – names redolent of the whole concept of northernness. It was appropriately grey and drizzly. The slate roofs were wet and shone in the rain, especially in Accrington, a primevally archetypal northern town with its rows of terraced houses spread out across the bowl of the valley and up the hillsides.

At Bilsborrow we were comfortably lodged at Olde Duncombe House with Mr and Mrs Bolton and sampled the Theakstons at The Roebuck (pricey and too chilled in my humble opinion). The one black spot on an otherwise promising horizon was the onset of foot problems – not Jane's this time but mine, and the first of the entire walk. It had been rank carelessness on my part. I'd felt something amiss on the long, 26-mile stint to Preston but had been too idle to investigate the problem. The result was the mother of all

135

blisters on the little toe of my right foot. I'd compounded the problem by not dealing properly with the toe during my weekend break. Giving medical treatment to one's own toes requires a back that bends and eyes that see and I am not 100 per cent in either of these departments. I consequently failed to diagnose that there was not one blister but three. It fell to Jane to try to repair the damage. Over the next few nights, recoiling from the dreadful smell, she struggled with dressings and blister pads in scenes reminiscent of a First World War casualty-clearing station. The wound appeared to have turned gangrenous and amputation was a distinct possibility.

Medical issues aside, the next few days were among the best of the whole walk. The weather was dry and clear without being swelteringly hot, and the going was generally easy. The Lancaster Canal heads due north from Preston for 40-odd miles through Lancaster to Tewitfield, just north of Carnforth. Jane and I spent Tuesday 30 May on the canal and reached Lancaster as planned. This particular section is the longest lock-free stretch of inland waterway in Britain – unsurprising given the flatness of the surrounding countryside. It wasn't a dramatic walk, but as the northern Lancashire coastal plain narrows, the canal is squeezed into contact with other main north-south transport arteries, the M6, the A6 and the main West Coast railway line. I thought the 110-foot aqueduct over the River Wyre was particularly impressive. It was completed in 1797 – a year earlier than the Dundas aqueduct which I'd enjoyed a month earlier in Somerset.

It was a beautiful evening for a walk around Lancaster. We went up to the priory and the castle, and looking north we had a clear view over Morecambe Bay. This was my first glimpse of the sea since I'd turned left at Porthleven and headed for Helston on day two of the walk. We could see over the bay to the mountains of the Lake District. They looked ... high. Another phase of the walk was about to begin.

More prosaically, but equally encouragingly, I caught most of England's first World Cup warm-up game – a straight-forward 3-1 win over Hungary.

Next morning the medical bulletins were more positive. Jane finally decided that amputation of my toe would not, after all, be necessary. The discomfort was manageable and we made an early start on another fine clear morning. My plan was to carry on along the canal, which crosses the river Lune on (another!) aqueduct, describes a spectacular loop to the south-west before heading north up to Carnforth. This was in turn part of the wider strategy of getting to Arnside and then linking up with two more long-distance footpaths, the Furness Way and the Cumbria Way, which would take me across the Lake District to Carlisle and thence into Scotland.

The plan was immediately disrupted by signs indicating the closure of the canal towpath just north of Lancaster. The revised route, improvised at very short notice, was shorter but less scenic. It brought us down off the canal into the Lune Valley Millennium Park and along a footpath by the river. A notice board on the path set out the park rules, one of which enjoined users to 'be polite and say hello to other walkers'. We duly proffered effusive greetings to the first walker we saw, an innocent lady out walking her dog. She was initially slightly alarmed and puzzled but soon managed to enter into the spirit of the thing.

We left the Lune at Halton and climbed the first hill since Staffordshire. This was definitely the end of the 'flat bit'. We could see whole ranges of Lake District mountains over to the north-west and, behind us, the view was back to Lancaster and as far as the nuclear power station at Heysham. In Nether Kellet we paused at the post office, the newsagents, the general store and at the local Tourist Information Centre. This actually took less time than might be supposed because all these operations were under one small roof and under the management of one exceptionally cheerful individual. We commented upon his one-man-band versatility and obvious crucial importance to the social fabric of the village. He agreed and, in order to demonstrate the full range of his abilities, offered to sing us a song as well.

We dropped down into Carnforth and lunched at the railway station visitor centre. It was here that David Lean's 1946 film *Brief Encounter* was made – the old buffet has been restored to more or less how it looked at the time with an old replica stove and period furniture. I had never seen the film, but the centre has it on a continuous loop, so the visitor can very quickly get an appreciation of what it's all about. Celia Johnson looked appropriately taut and dutiful, but somehow I couldn't quite buy into Trevor Howard in a role that cast him as a romantic hero. He was OK playing gnarled old soldiers and crusty admirals but the raincoat and trilby just weren't him at all. I soon left Jane to Trevor's tender loving care and went to look at the railway history section and the old memorabilia. Carnforth had been a real railway town in its day. In the early 1960s over 800 people had been employed at the station and maintenance shed.

We pressed on and had to walk for a short while along an unpleasantly busy stretch of road to Silverdale where we paused for afternoon tea and noted the extreme speed of the incoming tide. After Silverdale we left Lancashire and moved into Cumbria – I always felt a spurt of satisfaction at a new county – and came at around five o'clock into the small resort of Arnside at the head of Morecambe Bay. Arnside was a restful kind of place to be after a day's walking. A short promenade, a *very* short pier and two pubs selling decent beer. Jane and I chose the less busy of the two, Ye Olde Fighting Cocks, for fish and chips and (in my case) some Thwaites Lancaster Bomber.

From our bedroom window we had the view to Grange-over-Sands on the other side of the Kent Estuary and then to the peaks beyond. It held our attention for the whole of the long, slow, late-spring sunset. We sat happily taking photographs, trying to capture the subtle changes and gradations in the light and the gradual darkening of the hills. Every so often a train would cross the long bridge over the estuary and add its own small but satisfying dimension to the panorama.

If you ever chance to meet a Land's End–John O'Groat's walker whose chosen route includes the Lake District, ask him (or her) how they dealt with the Kent Estuary. It sounds like a very innocent question but note carefully any stumble or hesitation in the response. The River Kent flows south into Morecambe Bay and its estuary lies directly between Arnside and Grange-over-Sands. As the crow flies it's only about three miles between the two small towns. The rail journey lasts six minutes. But there's no road bridge over the estuary and if you look at a map you'll see that to do the journey by road takes vastly longer. The walker-friendly route that avoids the main roads actually takes the better part of two days. And, yes, you've guessed it, the ideal route for an end-to-ender through the Lake District goes precisely in that direction – north-west from Arnside, past Grange-over-Sands to the south of Lake Windermere before cutting up the eastern side of Coniston Water.

So Satan has presented the end-to-end walker with a choice. A two-day walk or a six-minute train ride. Which would *you* choose? I'm not aware of any set of formal rules as to what constitutes a valid end-to-end walk and what doesn't, but I'm sure that any putative LEJOG governing body or higher council would look pretty askance at that six-minute train ride.

I'd considered the whole issue very carefully. In line with my avowed aim of keeping the walk as direct and as efficient as possible I'd looked for other ways through the Lake District. I'd sought the expert opinion of Jeff and Rosemary (by this time they'd reached Inverness on their bikes) and had pored over my maps. The bottom line was that one *could* find more direct routes but only by using roads that, although probably meat and drink to Brian G. Smailes, were far too busy for the safety and comfort of ordinary walkers. And I had Jane to consider too. So I accepted that for once I'd have to go for the slow option.

The first two days on the Furness Way take the walker north to Crosthwaite and then due south again to Lindale and Cartmel – both about two miles from Grange-over-Sands. It was that second stage – a whole day walking due south to bring us back virtually to where we'd started – that was particularly galling. But never mind. This was the Lake District in early June. The weather was perfect. Just lie back and enjoy it.

Which we did. Jane insisted she was enjoying herself despite the onset of further pain in her feet. We'd only been on the road out of Arnside for half an hour or so the next morning before Jane's first pit stop. It was a lengthy one too. Off came the boots and the socks. Out came all the dressings and the various implements of foot repair and maintenance. It all looked desperately serious. I wasn't sure whether our travel insurance policy covered helicopter evacuation to the nearest hospital equipped with a specialist emergency chiropody unit.

Jane had picked up a blister during the long day's walk on the canal up to Lancaster and the constant impact of the walking was making matters worse. Eventually, to my relief the medical repair kit disappeared back into the rucksack.

We went through the Dallam Tower estate with its splendid parkland and walked up to Heversham. I was interested in the old well on the main street which was in use until 1908. Apparently at one stage it was contaminated by the old school privies, provoking an outbreak of typhoid among the infants and prompting the school to move up the road to Leasgill.

140

We went past the impressive Levens Hall, time pressures compelling us to forgo a visit to its world-famous topiary gardens, which were created as long ago as 1692, and are still impeccably maintained. Having resisted the temptation to cheat and cross the River Kent by rail, we now finally crossed it on foot and walked alongside it through more superb parkland – this time belonging to the Levens estate. On to yet another stately home, Sizergh castle, occupied for over 700 years by the Strickland family, and then the first moderately serious incline of the Furness Way up to Helsington church. From here we could see back to Arnside with its rail bridge, beyond to Morecambe Bay and, over to the north-west, the high peaks of the Lake District, including Great Gable and Scafell Pike. In front of us lay broad, green, Lyth Valley, home to the River Gilpin. It made for the kind of de luxe lunch venue that was compulsory when Jane was part of the expedition. I hadn't yet told her about Macclesfield bus station.

The trail edged north-west and then west past Brigsteer and Underbarrow to our night's resting place at Crosthwaite. Not a heavy day – 15 miles – in perfect weather and a supremely satisfying walk. In the evening we discovered that Crosthwaite boasted a real gastro-pub, the Punch Bowl, with a sophisticated menu and prices to match. The beer, Barnston's Westmorland Gold, was excellent. Even Jane had some.

Since Jane joined the trail in Preston I'd been successful in improving the standard of lunch venues and, in Lancaster, Arnside and Crosthwaite the evening places had been good too. Overall, I'd significantly upped my game on the organizational front and Jane had seemed fairly happy. But on Friday 2 June I messed up very badly indeed. Not only was there no lunch venue, there was actually no lunch either.

It was the day when we had to walk south and I'd assured Jane that before leaving Crosthwaite we'd be able to re-stock with supplies at the village post office-cum-shop. My Ordnance Survey map, which was relatively new (2005), and Andrew McCloy's book both made mention of this facility. But on arrival I found a team of builders busily converting the building from its former commercial use to residential premises. This was something of a setback – particularly in view of the rural and isolated nature of the day's walking. I hurriedly re-consulted the map and to my relief found that there was one potential source of salvation – a hotel at a place called Witherslack. It was some way to the south but at just about the point where we'd be ready for lunch. With a calm and easy confidence that I didn't really feel, I assured Jane that my initial cunning plan had a perfectly adequate fall-back and that there was absolutely no cause for alarm.

As the morning progressed and we climbed Whitbarrow Scar (706 feet) with excellent views back to Arnside (which looked gallingly close), I had the odd nagging stab of concern about lunch but the walk was so enjoyable and the air so balmy that the doubts were soon submerged beneath the general euphoria of the day. Unfortunately, as we descended Whitbarrow the mood began to darken. The sharpness of the descent plunged Jane's feet back into crisis; after a day's remission she suffered a relapse that, while not quite serious enough to warrant an air ambulance, made it essential that our lunch venue not only satisfied the usual exacting standards relating to view, privacy and general salubriousness but also provided an opportunity to examine feet. And, most crucially, good-quality restorative food and drink as well. As we neared Witherslack I crossed my fingers.

Witherslack is tiny – a small, leafy square bounded by the church and a few dwellings. I could tell immediately that we were out of luck. Where the hotel should have been was a house with a few children's toys littering the garden. I affected a mild grimace, stroked my chin and said 'OK' in the sort of tone that suggested acceptance of the impracticality of one idea but, simultaneously hinted of some deep-laid knowledge of other solutions to the problem. In reality I was totally clueless. The only solution that was occurring to me was the one adopted by the Uruguayan rugby team whose aircraft crashed somewhere deep in the Andes. Most of the team survived the crash but they were in a location almost as remote as Witherslack. When help finally arrived weeks later the rescue party found that the team was light of two prop forwards and a centre three-quarter but history doesn't record which it was that tasted better.

Strangely, it was Jane who came to the rescue. She opened her rucksack, pulled out a rather unprepossessing plastic bag and handed it to me.

'What the hell's that?' I said.

'It's scroggan,' she replied.

'And what the hell's *that*?' I said, my choice of vocabulary having crashed completely.

Scroggan, it turned out, is a form of Antipodean trail mix. It's designed for the sort of desperate situation that crops up occasionally in places like the Andes or Witherslack and is a mixture of compact but sustaining nutrients like raisins, chocolate and nuts. Jane had had this bag in the bowels of her rucksack ever since joining me for her first stint on the trail at Bath. Her view of the organizational ability of the average male (i.e. me) is such that she felt it necessary to carry her own fall-back position in case of emergency. And where had this stuff come from? Apparently from my daughter, whose assessment of male capabilities is probably, if anything, even lower than her mother's. My daughter had given it to Jane in the certain expectation of male organizational foul–up at some point on the walk.

The scroggan got us as far as Lindale where we found the post office. We bought food there but the owner, another Jane, took pity and made us a cup of tea – a sublime act of charity. It turned out that one of her friends was currently doing an end-to-end cycle ride.

Some food, taken on top of Jane's tea, got us up Hampsfell, which, at 727 feet, narrowly exceeded the day's previous highest at Whitbarrow. This was a spectacular view in the clear early evening light – most of the Furness coastline and a vast array of Lakeland peaks. And then down into Cartmel and the Cavendish Arms where I got stuck into the Jennings Cumberland bitter and we celebrated Jane's victory over another testing section of the end-to-end route. She planned to return home the following day and to rejoin me in Scotland if I made it that far.

Cartmel is a gem of a village. It has a wonderful 800-year-old priory and, amazingly, for a place of this size, a fully fledged racecourse. I particularly liked the market square, which is tight and intimate and architecturally superb.

We strolled around Cartmel in the dusk feeling very content. We'd survived the Witherslack episode and the pain in Jane's feet had soon receded once she'd stopped walking for the day. There was also good news on another metatarsal front. The media were full of a reported sighting of Wayne Rooney doing some running. It was all very vague and unconfirmed, in similar vein to 'sightings' of rare birds or pumas on Dartmoor, but it was an encouraging boost to England's World Cup prospects. Only one week to go. And I'd now reached the grand total of 609 end-to-end miles, which I thought was impressive until adding the P.S. that there was still around 500 more to cover before John O'Groats.

9

Enthusiasm must, on the whole, be counted a good thing. Far better to have someone approach a task with noisy gusto than tepid indifference. And the guy who'd written my guide book to the Furness Way was obviously an enthusiast. His name is Paul Hannon and he's a long-established writer/ photographer whose speciality is the upland areas of the British Isles. He has over 40 books behind him. Thus far I'd found his guide to the Furness Way indispensable because the trail had absolutely no waymarks whatsoever. The book was clear and accurate. But his enthusiasm was starting to jar a little.

I had time to reflect on such trivia because I now had nobody to talk to. Earlier that day I'd consigned Jane to the tender care of Nobby, Cartmel's cab driver, for the start of her journey home. I'd then climbed out of Cartmel onto the Ellerside Ridge and to my relief was now moving north again. Up on the ridge the topography on the ground differed from Hannon's directions but I didn't blame him for that. My edition was 12 years old and a lot can happen to the position of gates and fences in that time. No, my irritation stemmed from the fact that in Hannon's world it was always springtime. There were constant references in the book to bluebells as if they were a permanent feature of the landscape. And he had an annoying habit of investing inanimate objects with feelings and emotions, as well as a capacity for deliberate action. Trees, for example, were able to 'relent' and the village of Greenodd, he informed me 'waits patiently across the valley'. I did wish he'd stop doing that. And later in the day the River Crake was described as 'hapless'. How can a river be hapless for God's sake?

What had really pissed me off, though, was being told to 'continue in such fine fettle' the previous day on the descent from Hampsfell into Cartmel. How did *he* know what sort of fettle I was in? In fact I was in pretty *poor* fettle, my whole day's sustenance having consisted of two handfuls of scroggan.

I sensed the onset of one of my mutinous moods and resolved instead to enjoy another beautiful cloudless day. From the Ellerside Ridge I had a spectacular view westwards over the Leven Estuary to Ulverston (which Hannon told me was being 'watched over by the monument on Hoad Hill' – spare me, please).

I dropped down off the ridge and came across Bigland Tarn, the first actual lake on this, my third day in Lakeland. The descent brought me to the River Leven close to the village of Haverthwaite and I paused for lunch on the river bank. It was another of those moments on the walk that I wished I could bottle and take home. On the opposite bank I could see the village cricket team in action on a ground whose setting, bounded by trees and the river, was picture-postcard perfect. The only sounds as I sat in the sunshine were the buzzing of insects and the noise of leather on willow, with occasional muted shouts or languid ripples of applause. It was a grand walk, too, west alongside the broad River Leven to Greenodd, whose patience was now rewarded, through Penny Bridge and Spark Bridge by the River Crake. Which wasn't hapless in the slightest. I ended the day's walk at the village of Lowick Bridge and spent the night at the Red Lion.

I'd missed England's latest triumph that afternoon, a narrow, hard-fought 6-0 victory over mighty Jamaica, but saw the re-runs and enjoyed the privilege of having a bed some 10 vertical feet from the bar. I was drinking Hartley's XB, a beer that used to be brewed locally in the Lakes but is now produced in the more prosaic surroundings of Stockport. Connie, the landlady, and her team were immensely hospitable, although it occurred to me that the level of delegated authority granted to her husband gave him a degree of autonomy that necessitated a question, or request for authority to proceed, on average about every 15 seconds. Every minor issue relating to the food, the drink, or anything remotely related to the comfort of the guests, had to be referred to Connie. The bloke's room for manoeuvre was just about zero. But it all seemed to work fine and Connie very kindly made me a packed lunch the next morning as there was no prospect of finding any supplies before Coniston.

From Lowick Bridge the Furness Way picks a somewhat devious, arcane and potentially strenuous route to Coniston via Bethecar Moor and Grizedale Forest. But there's also a perfectly good secluded country road that runs straight and flat along the eastern shore of Coniston Water, and it took me all of two nanoseconds to plump for this latter option. And what a great decision it proved to be. It had been a dull start but the sun came out and the scenery blossomed as I moved north along the lakeside and the Old Man of Coniston hove gradually into view over to my left. It was Sunday morning and there was nobody around beside the odd cyclist.

The decision was even better for giving me the time and opportunity to visit Brantwood, which lies towards the northern end of Coniston Water almost opposite the town itself. Brantwood was the home of John Ruskin between 1872 and 1900. Prior to this visit I was hazy on Ruskin – dimly aware of his status as a major thinker of the Victorian era but very little else. 'Major thinker' is about right. As a relatively young man Ruskin became Britain's leading writer on culture and architecture but, on top of that, after 1850 he became a

147

political guru – a man whose ideas were way ahead of his time. He was an early supporter of socialism, champion of the working class and forceful challenger of the many and varied capitalist excesses of the time. All good stuff, but what I hadn't realized was that the poor guy also had an extremely interesting private life which seemed to deflect some of the attention of later generations away from his worthy efforts on the cultural and political front. His wife divorced him after six years, complaining that he had never consummated the marriage. She then ran off with the painter Millais, who was obviously a much better bet on the consummation front. Ruskin then, at the age of 40, met and fell in love with a ten-year-old girl, the enigmatically named Rose la Touche, but his proposal of marriage when the girl reached 18 was vetoed by her parents. She died a few years later leaving poor old Ruskin to a life punctuated by bouts of insanity and despair that culminated in total breakdown for the last ten years of his life.

There were two points about Ruskin that made me warm to him. He was a wealthy man, but he'd recognized the contradiction with socialist ideals and had given most of his money away. And he'd declined the offer of a grave in Westminster Abbey in favour of a plot in the churchyard at Coniston.

He was also a man with a good eye for property. The house and gardens at Brantwood are magnificent and occupy a sensational position above the lake.

I'd enjoyed Brantwood. I'd never heard of it before and was pleased that I'd taken the impulse decision to visit when I came across its signboard. One of the clinching factors behind my decision was recognizing the bloke behind the admission desk as last night's barman from the Red Lion. He greeted me like the proverbial long-lost friend. The walk was constantly providing surprises. This morning I'd barely heard of Ruskin and now I was an expert.

148

I whiled away a leisurely Sunday afternoon in Coniston. In the course of the walk there were several occasions when, after a sequence of rural days, I arrived in a larger town or known tourist destination and felt, in a small way, like a bloke who's just crossed the outback, or a Wild West gold prospector arriving in a frontier town after weeks in the mountains. It wasn't quite the same in that I didn't make straight for the saloon or the local whorehouse, but I appreciated the variety and choice of food and drink, and, in Coniston's case, the vast and comforting array of traditional Lakeland tourist tat in the shops.

I updated the blog after eight days of radio silence, made the acquaintance of Anne, the lady in the Tourist Office, who also turned out to be the Coniston NSPCC supremo, and then deliberated for hours as to whether to buy another pedometer to replace the Chinese lady who'd given up the ghost in Truro. I decided that a sufficiently long period of mourning had elapsed since her demise and invested what I felt was a slightly excessive £10.99 in a new (sadly voiceless) device.

I then went to the excellent little museum in Coniston, which has more Ruskin stuff, but which also deals well, indeed rather movingly, with Donald Campbell and his fatal accident on the morning of 4 January 1967, as he tried to set a new world water speed record. I hadn't appreciated that Campbell's body and the wreck of his boat weren't recovered until 2001. What was striking from the photographs and the old film footage was the glorious, British, amateurishness of Campbell's project. I know this was 1967 but I hadn't expected Bluebird to be housed in the kind of old shed where you'd normally expect to find a decrepit Austin Allegro. And there wasn't a sponsor's logo in sight.

That evening I went to The Sun. It's a pub/hotel slightly uphill out of Coniston, and it's where Campbell stayed during his attempts on the record. It wasn't as crowded as the other pubs and I sat on the terrace in the warm evening sunshine with the papers, a meal and some Hawkshead bitter. I'd enjoyed Coniston. I thought of Ruskin and Campbell – different characters in just about every conceivable way – but you could understand why the museum and the memorials are there and why Coniston claims the two men as its own.

From Coniston the Furness Way cuts west to Ravenglass on the coast. So here was another long-distance path that had outlived its usefulness and I had to find a replacement. It was time to switch to the Cumbria Way which approaches Coniston across the fells from Ulverston to the south. From Coniston it's then four days northwards across the heart of Lakeland to Carlisle.

Monday 5 June was my forty-eighth day on the road but I felt far from stale. Body and mind were in good shape – indeed if I could have looked into the future from Land's End I would probably have been quite surprised and delighted at my overall condition. I felt exuberant as I left Coniston that morning. It was fine and clear once again and the weather forecast was excellent. *The Times* seemed to share my exuberance and optimism. It had, if anything, got slightly carried away because it had decided to headline some deluded, asinine comments of Sven Goran Eriksson to the effect that England could beat Brazil and win the World Cup. The man was clearly losing his grip on reality.

England's first game of the competition was only five days away and I now had to give serious thought to where and how I was going to watch the games. By that time I'd be in Scotland. Would the England games be shown in a country whose World Cup prospects disappeared a long time ago and which was famously indifferent to the footballing fortunes of its southern neighbour? If the England games *were* transmitted would the pubs show them – or would there instead be a mulish and resentful insistence on changing channels to a more attractive domestic fixture like Alloa v Cowdenbeath? If the pubs *did* show the games would I have to sit mutely in a corner restraining all expression of partisanship? It was all rather tricky and worrying.

My first day on the Cumbria Way from Coniston to Dungeon Ghyll wasn't yet into the heavy duty Lakeland scenery and steep inclines of subsequent days. At Tarn Hows, which Paul Hannon rightfully labels 'one of Lakeland's most popular chocolate box scenes', there were notices warning about the dangers of slipping on the grass, which would surely have made the more rugged fell-walking denizens of Lakeland scoff with derision. It wasn't an unduly taxing day – north to the River Brathay and Skelwith Bridge and then a more north-westerly course to Elterwater and into the Langdale Valley. I stayed that night at the Old Dungeon Ghyll Hotel, an establishment apparently managed exclusively by adolescents from the far-flung corners of the EU, and it was there that I made a slightly alarming discovery.

While my blistered toe had now recovered, my right boot had, over the past ten days or so, been emitting an intermittent and at times irritatingly loud squeaking noise. Jane had commented upon it several times but it was only now that I subjected the boot to a proper visual inspection. All was not well. The heel was starting to detach itself from the main framework of the boot – there was a clear gap developing at the point where it met the upper. Total collapse didn't appear to be immediately imminent but it was still rather worrying.

I'd been taking my equipment for granted since Land's End. Some of it (like the boots) I'd acquired new for the walk and some at random points in the past, but it was all rather uncharismatic, workaday stuff. The only really interesting gadgets had been my much-lamented Chinese lady pedometer and the Wannabe Explorer compass that had been so invaluable on Bodmin Moor. But it was unnerving when an absolutely basic piece of equipment, something as

151

fundamental as a boot, started to misbehave and threaten to disintegrate.

I think the next day, Tuesday 6 June, and the walk from Dungeon Ghyll to Keswick, was probably the absolute high spot of the whole end-to-end project. Admittedly, it had competition, but this was the point where everything, the weather, the scenery, my improved state of fitness, all combined to make for the perfect walking day.

Walking up the Langdale Valley is like walking into a gigantic bowl. There's no visible way up any of the steep walls of rock that tower above you until you reach the very end of the valley and see Stake Pass. Hannon calls it 'this time honoured way linking Lakeland's best valleys of Langdale and Borrowdale'. It used to be a pack-horse route, but to deal with the heavy volume of modern-day walker traffic it's now a well-manicured zigzag path, that is actually quite easy going, with user-friendly steps and cobblestones.

From the top, at 1,575 feet on a clear day like this, the view is panoramic. The spot is a watershed, in that all water-courses encountered hitherto flowed south into Morecambe Bay by way of the Rivers Crake and Leven, whereas from here on they would flow north into Solway Firth via the Caldew or the Derwent. The way down into Langstrath was a lot harder than the way up, and walking along the valley floor I complained bitterly into my Dictaphone that the path was strewn with scree and boulders that presented all kinds of opportunities to fall over. Within two minutes I'd met a poor guy who'd done precisely that and was nursing a lacerated arm. It set me wondering again, although only briefly thank goodness, about guide books. Rather than the usual tone of unquenchable optimism adopted by Hannon and his ilk why not something a little more honest and realistic? Personally, if it was my book, at this juncture I would have said something along the lines of 'by now you'll be feeling pretty knackered and this poxy path will, quite understandably, be starting to seriously piss you off'.

It didn't last for long. After a while Langstrath makes a 90-degree left turn and becomes Borrowdale. Whereas Langdale is craggy and imposing, Borrowdale is greener, with meadows and woodland. It was here that I received final confirmation of the total incompatibility between me and pedometers. It was clear we just weren't meant for each other. This was the second day of operation of the new device that I'd agonized over in Coniston. It had worked perfectly thus far, but as I stood on the bridge over Stonethwaite Beck, drinking in the view, I noticed that the clip attaching it to my waistband had fallen slightly open. I put my hand down to fix it, only to see the pedometer detach itself completely, bounce on the wooden floor of the bridge and arc gracefully into the water. Another 'Air on a G String' moment. This was the third pedometer I'd had in a matter of weeks (the Chinese lady had been a replacement for a device that steadfastly refused to function as soon as I got it home).

Undeterred by this crushing setback I pressed on to the hamlet of Stonethwaite – an idyllic little spot containing a pub/hotel, a teashop, several cottages and a farmhouse set behind the absolute epitome of the English country garden. Was the place real? It was so perfect that, in retrospect, I begin to wonder. I'd like to go back one day and check.

After lunch I walked on through the village of Rosthwaite and joined the River Derwent. Another idyll. There were folk swimming and it was tempting to join them. The trail passed between the 'jaws' of Borrowdale, the imposing entrance to the valley between Castle Crag and Grange Fell. And then the final leg of the day, a leisurely winding path through the woods along the bays and promontories of Derwentwater. It had been a jewel of a day. When I reached Keswick it was frontier town time again and I topped it all off with a curry.

The following day was almost as good. A steep climb out of Keswick up the slopes of Skiddaw with views back over

Derwentwater and, to the west, Bassenthwaite Lake. I can't recall ever experiencing better light quality in the United Kingdom. It was Alpine in its clarity and sharpness. The Cumbria Way then turned due north up the deep and narrow Glenderaterra Valley – in bare and treeless contrast to Borrowdale and Derwentwater – before reaching Skiddaw House which, at 1,542 feet, has the distinction of being Lakeland's highest habitable stone building. It's actually a rather grim-looking house in a forbiddingly isolated location. Its chequered history has included spells as a shepherd's bothy, a schools' outdoor centre and a youth hostel but it's been empty since 2003. I'm not surprised frankly. It's a hell of a spot to find you've run out of cornflakes.

From Skiddaw House there's a choice of paths and I opted for the 'direct' one – shorter, but involving what turned out to be quite a rugged and difficult scramble alongside a beck up to High Pike, which at 2,158 feet is the highest point on the Cumbria Way and also, coincidentally, the highest on my end-to-end route. I wasn't geographically aware enough to realize, until I reached the summit, that I'd just completed my walk through Lakeland. Away to the north (it was still breathtakingly clear) the view sloped dramatically away to lowland, with farms and fields almost as far as the eye could see, and then beyond, just a hint of the hills of Southern Scotland. The realization felt good. As did the quick and easy descent into the village of Caldbeck.

I enjoyed Caldbeck. It's the most northerly village in the Lakeland National Park and is something of a Luddite's paradise. There's no mobile phone reception at all, and even better, the place boasts a traditional clog-maker. His name, in case you're interested, is Joe Stone. How good a name is *that*? I went to the Oddfellows Arms for my Jennings Cumberland bitter and felt very content.

I'd actually had difficulty finding accommodation in Caldbeck and had ended up accepting an offer to spend the night in a caravan situated in the front garden of the redoubtable Mrs Savage at Swaledale Watch. I'd never stayed in a caravan before and I was curious to see how it felt. To a certain extent it was a controlled experiment because I didn't eat in the caravan and Mrs Savage kindly gave me unfettered access to the luxury bathroom facilities inside her house. But, controlled or not, the experiment yielded some interesting results.

The caravan's closeness to nature proved something of an irritant when I was woken by the cacophonous dawn chorus at 4 a.m. But the sleeping side of things was fine. What did prove something of an eye-opener, though, were the ablution facilities. The arrangement I'd reached with Mrs Savage obviated the need for me to actually use them in a 'live fire' situation, but I nevertheless staged a realistic simulation. Obviously, my lack of experience of caravans was a handicap – as indeed were my size and my inelastic backbone – but I found it almost impossible to even get into the 'bathroom', let alone actually use it in anger. It was about half the size of its counterpart on a commercial jet aircraft. When I'd finally managed to squeeze into it, not only was closing the door a complete impossibility, but I found myself contorted into a kind of twisted semi-crouch that would have made Quasimodo look relaxed and supple by comparison. Having got this far I looked around for clues as to the next step. I then realized that I was being invited to use something called a Thetford Porta Potti. The mind reeled.

I regret to say that it was at this juncture I called a halt to the simulation. Actually using the Porta Potti would have entailed feats of agility that I hadn't achieved in years, and my back was already in some pain.

Interesting, though, and for the sake of completeness I should record that if I'd persisted with the experiment, I could have tried the fold-down sink – or even the shower. Although, on reflection, if I hadn't sufficient dexterity to manage the Porta Potti, getting to grips with the shower had to be regarded as a complete impossibility.

I actually went to the trouble of looking up the Thetford Porta Potti on the Internet. I was worried that, like Stonethwaite, it might just have been the residual fragment of a dream. But no, it was there all right. It's obviously a very robust and effective product. I checked the accompanying commentary, which informed me that 'Features include pressure release button [and] integrated swivelling pour and spout (for splash free emptying)'. Moreover, the Porta Potti boasts a 'powerfully effective fresh water flush, a snap-lock system that allows water and waste holding tanks to be connected and taken apart easier (sic) than ever'.

I think it was when I came to the bits about 'splash free emptying' and the 'taking apart of water and waste tanks' that my enthusiasm for caravans, already extremely fragile, collapsed completely.

Mrs Savage provided an excellent breakfast and gave me a donation for the NSPCC. She told me twice that I would make it to John O'Groats. 'You will do it,' she said in a soft, cosseting, complacent tone, and then a few seconds later it was 'You WILL do it.' This time it was an order.

Before leaving Caldbeck on the morning of Thursday 8 June I went to the churchyard and located the grave of John Peel – not the broadcaster but the Cumberland huntsman immortalized in song.

The last stage of the Cumbria Way, 14 miles from Caldbeck into Carlisle, is gentle compared to the previous two days. The path climbs out of Caldbeck to 580 feet – trifling in a Lakeland context but enough elevation to give me a last, nostalgic look back at the high fells. Afterwards there's a descent to the River Caldew and the trail follows it north towards Carlisle. I lunched at Dalston and in the afternoon I found the Cumbria Way diminished to the status of a metalled cycle track alongside the Barrow in Furness to

Carlisle railway line. It's rather an anti-climax for a trail that's led such an aristocratic and interesting life.

I didn't mind in the slightest. Arriving in Carlisle was an obvious and gratifying punctuation mark on the end-to-end trail. To my amazement I'd just walked the length of England. I only had one more country to go.

10

I hadn't given much thought to Southern Scotland during my initial route planning. I'd been so carried away by the brilliance of my Bollin Valley/Lancashire canals/Lake District strategy that I'd given only minimal thought to what was to follow. From the perspective of Land's End, Carlisle was so far into the future (691 miles to be precise) as not to merit detailed consideration. I did have a plan of sorts but it was sketchy and relied on unproven assumptions. The time had now come to put these assumptions to the test.

Between Carlisle and Glasgow there's around 100 miles of sparsely populated terrain with no long-distance footpaths apart from the Southern Upland Way, which follows a completely unhelpful east–west course. It's an anti-climax after the grandeur of Lakeland and all its scenic and well-documented footpaths. End-to-end walkers, perhaps the majority, who have opted to follow the Pennine Way, are spared Carlisle–Glasgow because the Pennine Way has taken them up through the Cheviots, considerably further north into Scotland, and Andrew McCloy then finds them a comfortable route across to the north of Glasgow to join the West Highland Way. McCloy's 1994 book does suggest a potential route up from Carlisle but somehow his description lacks conviction. You can tell his heart isn't in it. In answer to the question 'How do I get to Glasgow?' McCloy, in effect, gives the splendid Irish response 'If you want to go to Glasgow don't start from here.'

But things have changed in this part of the world since 1994. The main highway up to Glasgow was the A74. In recent times, however, this has metamorphosed into the A74M and it was this change that gave me the basis of my sketchy plan. It seemed to my untutored eye that it hadn't merely been a case of upgrading the road. The planners had gone the whole hog and built a brand-new motorway, leaving the old A74 to languish and fade into obscurity with a down-market new identity as the B7076. Furthermore, in pensioning off the old A74, the planners had sprinkled a whole set of green dots along its course on my Ordnance Survey map. The green dots were code for cycle track, a designation given only to roads with light or non-existent traffic, and therefore a hospitable environment for bikers (and crucially, as experience was teaching me, for walkers too).

So having scornfully rejected Brian G. Smailes and his use of main roads, I was now planning to incorporate part of his strategy into my own. The problem was that my idea of a quick four-day sprint up the road to Glasgow had not yet found favour with (or as far as I could determine, even been tested by) any of the great LEJOG gurus or other opinion shapers in the wonderful world of walking. But then I met Dave in Carlisle.

Dave was a fellow guest at my B&B and the first end-to-ender I'd met since saying farewell to Roy and Maureen in Launceston. He was walking north–south and was making very good time. He was English, and part of his motivation for moving fast was a desire to be over the border in England before the World Cup got under way. He shared my concern at the potential difficulty of following England's campaign in the less hospitable environment north of the border. (And here was me *leaving* England the day before their first game.)

Of course, having discovered that we were both end-to-enders, our first topic of conversation was the all-consuming subject of routes. The boredom factor for any eavesdropper

159

would have been way off the scale, but Dave and I both found the conversation useful and extremely stimulating. Dave seemed very receptive to the Bollin Valley Way concept and I in turn was delighted that he ringingly endorsed my plan for Southern Scotland. He was also very useful on the subject of Glasgow. Here was another substantial potential barrier to the aspiring end-to-ender. Dave said he'd tried to find a route, championed on various occasions by McCloy, which uses country parks and disused railway lines, but he'd become hopelessly lost. He'd found himself in an area of vandalized tower blocks where the only living things to be seen at ground level staggered around clutching half-empty bottles of Famous Grouse. He may have been exaggerating – or there again maybe he wasn't. 'Just go straight through the middle' was his advice.

To my amazement Dave told me he was doing the walk without maps. Whether this idea stemmed from a lack of funds or just sheer bravado wasn't clear, but I thought this was extremely impressive – and an excellent way of meeting people.

We also, of course, analysed England's World Cup prospects, taking heart from the successful outcome of a scan undergone by Wayne on the famous metatarsal the previous day. This had necessitated our hero flying back from the team's base in Baden Baden to Manchester for the day, his every mile being remorselessly tracked by the world's media. It had been reminiscent of O.J. Simpson's ride down the freeway.

I was grateful to Dave for reminding me about Glasgow. I'd had a cunning plan for dealing with the city for several months, but suddenly, now that Glasgow was only a few days away, I thought it was time to nail the strategy down.

My cunning plan for dealing with Glasgow wasn't really a plan at all. It was a person – Peter to be exact. Months

160

before, when the whole end-to-end project was still on the drawing board, my friend Peter had announced his firm and unalterable intention of riding shotgun with me through Glasgow. Peter is a Scot who spent much of his youth in Glasgow, and he felt that his local knowledge would be an invaluable source of support. He was going to guide me through the city and act as my local bearer and interpreter.

The problem with all this was that Peter doesn't live in Glasgow. He lives very close to me in Norwich. His offer of support was extremely welcome to me, but for him it entailed a round trip of some 900 miles on a date that I couldn't accurately predict – all for the sake of two days' predominantly urban, and distinctly unscenic, walking. Not to mention, of course, the almost certain prospect of significant pain and discomfort. It was way above and beyond the call of duty. I'd tried on several occasions to dissuade him from this madcap idea, but Peter's resolve had thus far been absolutely unbending. Nevertheless, I thought it was time to talk to Peter again because there was now another compelling reason for my wanting him to join me.

I'd anxiously checked the state of my right boot every night since initially discovering the onset of its structural disintegration. Each inspection revealed a further small but discernible deterioration. But if the boot could hold out for another four or five days, relief would be at hand in the shape of the back-up pair currently languishing at home. And Peter would make an ideal courier.

I wished Dave good luck and headed north out of the city. It was Friday 9 June and it promised to be baking hot. I should mention that Carlisle had been especially noteworthy for the vast quantity of flags. They were hanging everywhere – cars, pubs, houses – in concentrations that far exceeded any other place I'd visited en route. Maybe it was because Carlisle is a frontier town and the people felt more of a need to demonstrate their allegiance than those in other more central locations.

161

Actually Carlisle isn't *quite* on the frontier. Longtown, about 7 miles to the north, is even closer to the border, and the bunting and flags here were even more numerous than those in Carlisle. It was heartwarming because I knew full well I wouldn't be seeing many (any?) St George flags from now on.

The terrain north of Carlisle was flat and uninspiring. I seemed to walk a long way without the benefit of shade. At Longtown I crossed the River Esk and turned westwards towards Gretna along the A6071. This was the first sustained piece of walking along a main highway since a short burst in Somerset north of Glastonbury. There was a path for a while then a grass verge of sorts, but this was not a pleasant 3 miles. Either side of the road lies the Longtown Ammunition Depot. For obvious reasons there is a distinct limit to what one can see from the road, but it looks bleak and forbidding – certainly not the British Army's most glamorous posting. 'Oh no Sarge, please, not Longtown. Please. I much prefer it here in Basra.'

Before reaching Gretna I fell prey to profound and irre-sistible hunger, so with my unerring eye for an uncomfortable lunch venue I found another farm whose wall I could stand next to. This one was called Plumpe Farm. The venue was so skilfully selected that within about 30 seconds and 100 yards of heaving on the rucksack and departing I was heaving the rucksack off again and taking photographs of the sign that welcomed me to Scotland. Naturally, there was a magnificent bench right by the sign which would have been perfect for lunch – it would even have met Jane's exacting requirements.

It was good to be in Scotland. Crossing the border some-how made me feel refreshed and sharper and I immediately looked for differences, for manifestations of Scottishness. I was at once rewarded by the sight of some Highland cattle, staring balefully at me from a field that probably belonged to Plumpe Farm. They were quite photogenic in a way, but as this wasn't even the Lowlands yet, let alone the Highlands, I kept the camera in my pocket. Predictably, of course they were the last Highland cattle I saw on the entire walk.

The road skirted round Gretna to the north and it would have required something of a detour to visit the town. So I resisted instructions to visit the 'World Famous Blacksmith's Forge' and pressed on. In any case I was in a hurry now. I had a deadline to meet. England's first World Cup game was due to kick off some 24 hours hence at 2 p.m. the next day, and in the course of the morning I'd secured accommodation, complete with television, in Lockerbie, some 17 miles distant. I wanted to be safely ensconced in front of that TV well before kick off in order to have time to savour the big-match atmosphere. I'd been assured that I'd been extremely fortunate to find a room in Lockerbie as it was 'Gala Day'.

The road passed very close to Quintinshill, the site of Britain's worst-ever train disaster. We sometimes moan about our modern-day health and safety regime. Reading accounts of this accident makes one realize just how far we've progressed – although signalmen reading the newspaper and failing to notice a train standing directly in front of them, not to mention passengers locked in old wooden coaches lit by gas, were probably not particularly flash even by the standards pertaining on 22 May 1915. Some 230 people were killed in the accident and resultant fire – most of them soldiers of the 7th Royal Scots on their way to the Dardanelles.

Bed-and-breakfast accommodation in this part of the world was scarce and I'd had to settle for a relatively expensive motel establishment in Kirkpatrick Fleming, a few miles north-west of Gretna. I arrived there at around 3 p.m. and decided it would be a shame to stop walking for the day, particularly as I had my football deadline to meet. I therefore did a deal with a splendid local cab driver called Elaine. I would walk further along the B7076 towards Lockerbie, she

163

would collect me and return me to the motel when I asked to be rescued and then drive me back to the same spot early the next day.

The arrangement worked perfectly. What I hadn't bargained for, however, was the magical effect of removing the rucksack. I left it at the motel and, relieved of a burden that had become an indissoluble part of my anatomy for over 700 miles, the legs accelerated from their customary leaden trudge to what seemed, by comparison, a giddying headlong sprint. Elaine couldn't respond immediately to my call for help and by the time she arrived I'd plunged on at breakneck speed in the baking heat to a point way beyond Kirtlebridge. There was an entertaining dimension to the afternoon in the shape of a variety of local motorists who stopped and generously offered me a lift. I'm sure they must have been puzzled by my declinature of their kind offers on the grounds that acceptance would infringe the rules of a Land's End–John O'Groats walk. They must have wondered how on earth this scruffy Englishman was going to walk that far without a vestige of luggage to his name, but they were all far too polite to comment.

These conversations, following on that with Elaine and the very helpful lady at the motel, got me wondering about accents. How was it that within a space of about 3 miles the accent could change so radically? There was a world of difference between the rugged northern English of Longtown and the clipped, lilting Scottish of Kirkpatrick Fleming. And yet there was no major physical barrier between the two, no great impediment to normal commercial and social intercourse – or any other kind of intercourse come to that. So why did 3 miles of road entail such a major shift in the way people spoke? I was baffled.

The additional miles I covered that afternoon were encouraging. The inroads I'd made into the next day's walking meant that the football deadline would, with the continued assistance of Elaine, be easily achievable. But I was also heartened by the nature of the road itself – straight, minimal traffic and a clearly marked lane for the use of cyclists and walkers. It boded well for the days ahead. So I was in good heart when I got back to the motel and settled down to catch up with the official opening of the World Cup and the first actual game.

That night I attempted the first few faltering steps towards one of the subsidiary objectives I'd set myself to achieve during the walk. I wanted to solve the mystery of Scottish beer. Now, of course most people, especially Scots, clarify this whole issue to their entire satisfaction in the first few minutes of their drinking careers. But somehow I'd got left behind. My previous visits to Scotland had been so short and infrequent, and my opportunities for serious imbibing so restricted, that I was very hazy on such crucial issues as what was 'heavy', what was 'light' and why so much of the beer is apparently denominated in 'shillings'. I entered the motel bar eagerly anticipating my first pint north of the border and the opening shots in what I hoped would be a sustained and well-executed campaign of research.

The only beer they had on offer was something called Thwaites 'Smooth'. Now the Thwaites that I know is a Blackburn-based brewery which turns out some quite decent real beers. Was this the same Thwaites? And what was this 'smooth' stuff? I asked the bloke behind the bar. Unfortunately, his knowledge of the product he was selling was depressingly scant and he couldn't enlighten me on either score. Nothing daunted, I decided to have a go at the 'smooth'. It evidently represented another, hitherto unknown, dimension to Scottish beer and would be a good place to start my research.

And the beer wasn't bad. The trouble was it wasn't good either. It was just completely and utterly tasteless. Hard though I tried, my taste buds remained totally unengaged. It

165

was like drinking liquid cardboard. Huge amounts of hard work and ingenuity must have gone into devising and building the process of taste removal through which this beer had so carefully and so lovingly been passed.

I wondered if the 'smooth' had a counterpart. After all there's bitter and mild, pale ale and brown ale and (in Scotland at least) heavy and light. Maybe there was a cask of Thwaites 'rough' tucked round the back somewhere, only made available for use when there were serious drinkers in the vicinity. I thought maybe I'd ask for a pint of 'rough' after the football tomorrow and see what happened. But clearly nothing was going to happen if I continued drinking the 'smooth' so I stopped and resorted to Guinness, the old standby when all else fails.

It was a disappointing start to my research campaign but I did manage to solve one small mystery before the end of the day. Earlier I'd been baffled by the insistent signs that had urged me to visit the Blacksmith's Forge in Gretna. There was a large wedding party staying in the hotel and I remembered, of course, about Gretna's wedding industry. In the days when the difference between English and Scottish law impelled desperate young marriage-seeking English couples to elope to Gretna, it was often the village blacksmith who performed the ceremony. This was because the blacksmith was at the heart of the local community and usually held in correspondingly high regard. The law now allows couples to marry wherever they choose, but recently the tradition of 'anvil' weddings has been revived, with the minister performing the ceremony over the anvil outside church premises – often at the Old Smithy itself. Apparently around one Scottish wedding in eight now takes place in Gretna.

So the big day dawned – 10 June and England's opening World Cup game against those giants of world football, Paraguay. Elaine duly pitched up on time and deposited me back at the precise point on the road where she'd picked me up the previous evening. Before we parted we engaged in a bizarre and complex species of reciprocal donation session where Elaine gave to the NSPCC and I favoured the hospice which she supports via a variety of activities including sponsored walks and runs. Elaine was one lovely, feisty lady, another of the many brief encounters that gave the walk so much spice and interest.

I carried on along the B7076. There wasn't a great deal to see and do other than to watch as my road, the accompanying motorway and the main West Coast railway line constantly changed places, weaving over and under each other as they ran north-west towards Lockerbie. I passed through Ecclefechan, the birthplace of the nineteenth-century writer Thomas Carlyle, and over a river enigmatically called The Water of Milk. It was a hot day and I was pleased I'd set up an early finish.

I walked into Lockerbie around 11.30 to find the main street lined with people standing three or four deep. I'd forgotten about Gala Day. I realized that not only was I in time for the football, I was also just in time for the Gala Day procession. So I took up a position just up from the railway station and awaited developments with interest.

The procession started with a pipe band. Thoroughly logical and appropriate in the circumstances. It then continued with a succession of floats and other random items that were of obvious local interest but whose significance was at least partially lost on the English visitor. The pace of the procession was funereal. It would halt for minutes on end while some obstruction further up the road was cleared before grinding on again in the baking heat.

I was mildly surprised to note that the third item in the procession was also a pipe band. And then, rather depressingly, the fifth as well. As the procession wore on it became clear that every alternate item was going to be a pipe band. The bullet-headed son of Lockerbie standing beside me, pint of lager in hand, was finding it hard to conceal his irritation. As each new band hove slowly into view I would hear the words 'Not another f****** pipe band' issue gutturally from my left, followed by a string of further unfavourable comment on Gala Day and its organizers.

The procession seemed to go on for ever. Interspersed amongst the pipe bands were the float carrying the Gala Queen, some tractors, a lot more floats and a collection of classic cars, among which, quite inexplicably, was a thoroughly modern-day Lexus. I couldn't quite see the point of the tractors either. At some bleak moment several hours into the procession I wondered darkly whether ownership of a tractor was all it took to qualify for inclusion – maybe a tractor was still considered a sufficiently novel and interesting device to merit a place in the parade. The man on my left had long since gone to replenish his lager.

There was an opportunity for partial redemption in the shape of a float belonging to the local dance academy. A few shapely tutus would have improved things no end, for me at least, even though the man with the lager had, by this time, lost all interest and disappeared to the pub. But the opportunity was wasted. The tutus were rather middle-aged, and failed to rekindle the interest of a, by now, jaded and slightly restive crowd.

So it was with some relief that I went across the square and checked into the Kings Arms. I drew the curtains against the harsh light and the seventy-fourth rendition of 'Scotland the Brave' and hunkered down to watch the football.

I emerged blinking into the sunlight some two hours later. There was still the odd residual pipe band around but the place had quietened down somewhat. After all the hype and expectation the afternoon had, of course, been a complete waste of time. I would have been much better employed eating up a few more miles on the B7076. And the really frustrating thing was that I knew, despite all this, that

168

tomorrow I'd begin making careful preparations to ensure that I didn't miss England's next game against those even bigger giants of world football, Trinidad and Tobago.

I tried to still my frustrations with a visit to Lockerbie's library, which had, amazingly, re-opened after the procession. I needed to do some urgent research into Glasgow. I'd called Peter who, to my surprise, had confessed total ignorance of routes through the city. However, he was hopeful that his brother Gilbert might be able to help. This news was mildly discouraging. I'd pinned my hopes on Peter having a particularly cunning plan up his sleeve, but it was now clear that neither of us had the remotest idea as to the best place to rendezvous, the most suitable potential accommodation or where we were going to walk. I got out a few maps and gazetteers and set to work in the library which, apart from me, was completely empty.

It turned out OK in the end. I worked out a plan, which, whilst not especially cunning, would do for starters. As I left the library the skirl of the pipes on yet another rendition of 'Scotland the Brave' could still be heard in some distant benighted quarter of the town.

It's around 62 miles from Lockerbie up to Larkhall on the south-eastern approaches to Glasgow. It took three days to cover this ground – all along roads which were the descendants of my old friend the B7076. They looked much the same and behaved in much the same way. It's remote territory and the only real problem I encountered was boredom. Nothing much would happen on the road for hours. Even a passing car would be sufficient to create interest, while a road junction or signpost could provoke wild excitement. I wished I'd been able to develop a technique for reading or doing sudoku while I walked but I was scared of falling over. To pass the time I played memory games (the 50 places I'd stayed since leaving Land's End) or counted the seconds between a vehicle passing me and disappearing over the horizon (the record was about a minute and a half).

I spent a night at Moffat. It was Sunday afternoon when I arrived and I expected a dour, Calvinist sort of place, all firmly closed and buttoned down for the Sabbath. But I couldn't have been more wrong. The Black Bull was open and was doing a roaring trade, the shops were busy and so was the Rumblin' Tum tearoom where I settled down for a cup of tea, a piece of fruit cake and a look at the Scottish edition of the *News of the World*. And it got better. The museum had just closed but there was an excellent souvenir shop where I derived great comfort from the fact that, should I wish to, I could still, after all these years, get CDs by Andy Stewart, Sir Harry Lauder, Kenneth McKellar and Jimmy Shand. Of course I'd absolutely no desire or intention to buy this kind of stuff. But it was just comforting to know that I still could – and that, in a rapidly changing world, there are still a few rock-solid, constant points of reference to cling on to. Then the man in the Texaco service station sold me a map and improved my mood even further by making a very generous donation to the NSPCC. A further attraction was a 'Tarot Evening' at the Buccleugh Arms later in the week featuring 'tarot, runes and healing'. There really was far more going on in Moffat than I'd anticipated.

After my disappointing false start in the bar of the motel at Kirkpatrick Fleming, Moffat gave me the opportunity to do some solid research into Scottish beer. The Black Bull opened in 1683 and Robert Burns called there once. I tried the Deuchars IPA and then the McEwans 80 Shilling, both tolerable real ales, if a little sweet for my liking. The B&B in Moffat was good too. Mhairi must have been the youngest landlady of the entire walk by at least ten years.

I really savoured my *Scottish News of the World*. It contained an extensive description of the (allegedly) less than illustrious early phases of Heather Mills' career, but the main focus of my attention and amusement was the way in which it dealt with the football. It was the match between Sweden and Trinidad that was the subject of the main sporting banner headline. A much smaller, subsidiary headline said '. . . And England win too'. A very wry and pleasant way of putting the English in their place. Trinidad were rivals of England in the same preliminary group and Neil, another Scottish friend, gleefully informed me that the supply of replica Trinidad shirts in Scotland had long since sold out. You couldn't get one now for love nor money. I asked him whether he'd seen the England game on TV. He said he hadn't, as family and friends would not have considered it 'good form'.

After Moffat the scenery becomes bleaker as the road climbs towards Beattock summit. It was here that it rained – the first time since Wilmslow. The cloud base was at or close to the tops of the conifers for most of the morning. The walker now had the River Annan as an occasional companion to complement the motorway and the railway. But not much else. The tedium was broken on one occasion by an RAF Tornado that suddenly appeared round the edge of a nearby hill, standing on its wingtip, and screamed over my head at deafeningly low altitude.

I lunched at the absolute precise apogee of Beattock summit. The trains were climbing as they approached me and descending as they went away. The Virgin electric trains appeared to be making short work of the incline. I reflected that lunch on the same spot 50 years ago would have been accompanied by the rather louder and more exciting sound of steam locomotives hauling heavy London–Glasgow express trains to the summit.

After Beattock summit the road descends and, close to the hamlet of Elvanfoot, meets the infant River Clyde. I spent the night at the motorway service station at nearby Abington – not exactly the highlight of the walk but the only accommodation I could find that was remotely close to my route.

I ploughed on in similar mode the next day, Tuesday 13 June, but the boredom factor was even higher now. The minimal sources of interest that *had* been present over the last two days, namely the accompanying motorway and the railway, were now nowhere to be seen. The only major event in hours was a gravel works. For long spells the road was a dual carriageway, and for equally long spells I was its sole occupant. The traffic count had declined from very occasional to non-existent. I amused myself by walking in the outside lane, then on the central reservation. The road climbed steadily again and even the trees disappeared.

Actually I wasn't that unhappy. I could do boring very easily as long as it was straight and was getting me places. And this road was certainly doing that. By late morning I was descending, and as the weather cleared there was the distinct hint of lower, flatter ground ahead. Just before midday a major event. A T-junction and a motorway interchange. This was the road from Ayr, joining from the west, and from this point the pace of life quickened perceptibly. The road from here was busier, although there was still a well-marked cycle path, and then, wonder of wonders, a pub! It was not the most enticing hostelry I'd ever seen: in fact, the gravitational pull it exerted was relatively weak, but it was the first roadside pub I'd seen in ages and a sign that the doldrums of Southern Scotland were almost behind me.

I arrived in the small town/big village of Lesmahagow feeling like a man who's just crossed the Kalahari Desert. Apart from a few houses at Abington this was the first civilization I'd seen in a day and a half and I gazed with wonder at such novelties as the tanning salon and the take-away curry shop. I paused for lunch outside Lesmahagow's extensive, well-maintained cemetery and carried on.

Blackwood was the next place and it was here that the benign green dots on the map came to a halt, indicating that the road was no longer part of the national network of cycle

172

tracks. Within five minutes I was yearning for the boring but extremely safe roads that had brought me northwards from the border. There was one particularly tricky section where heavy lorries thundered past within inches of the rucksack as I cowered in the hedge but I was soon rescued by a long and intricate series of roadworks which necessitated single-lane working and enabled me to walk unimpeded for long stretches down the part of the carriageway that was being repaired. The guys driving the big road surfacing machines didn't seem to mind in the slightest and by the time the roadworks had finished I was walking on a pavement and approaching the outskirts of Larkhall.

A glance at the map shows Larkhall's position at the extreme south-eastern corner of the Glasgow conurbation. It was here that I planned to meet Peter, and it was from here that we'd launch our assault on the city the following day. It was still only mid-afternoon, and enthused by the success of the scheme that I'd put into practice with Elaine's help back in Kirkpatrick Fleming, I decided to walk through Larkhall and make a few inroads into the miles we'd need to cover the next day.

I suppose it's only human nature to wish for something that is manifestly not obtainable in the place you happen to be at the time. Crossing the Sahara Desert, it would be quite natural to pine for an English-style pub beside a gently flowing river. In the Antarctic you might yearn for tanning salons and take-away curry shops. That afternoon in Larkhall I developed a forlorn and desperate longing for a cosy little tearoom – the kind of genteel and comfortable establishment where the crew, and, come to think of it, the clientele, are all cheerfully polite and well-spoken, middle-aged ladies. The only difference being that the crew might wear carefully ironed white pinafores. You know the kind of place. Nice chunky pottery plates and teapots. Big helpings of cream with the scones.

Normally, of course, I wouldn't look twice at such a place. I'd probably walked past dozens already in the course of the walk without a second thought. Not that I didn't like them – quite the reverse. It was just that the arrival in the midst of the tearoom's well-dressed and pleasantly coiffured clientele of a large, ungainly, ageing hobo, smelling like a goat, was not calculated to improve anyone's afternoon.

But I really fancied scones and cream that afternoon and, of course, Larkhall was the last place I was going to find them. What I did find, though, when I paused to buy a palliative chocolate bar, was the most heavily fortified shop I'd ever seen. Sure, in any English city, iron grilles and bars on the windows are commonplace, but I'd never seen barbed wire on a shop roof before. The place looked totally unkempt and abandoned, but when I pushed gently at the door it opened to reveal a smart, newly fitted, well-lit general store managed by a very personable guy of Indian extraction. The dimensions were deceptive too. It was rather like Dr Who's Tardis – much bigger inside than its external appearance indicated.

Throughout all this long day, of course, during my encounters with tanning salons, cemeteries and Tardis-style general stores, Peter had been on the road up from East Anglia. When it eventually came, our rendezvous at the northern edge of Larkhall, at the entrance to the Chatelherault Country Park, had required a degree of organization that made the docking of the space shuttle with the Mir space station look like a casual and impromptu piece of off-the-cuff improvisation.

We enjoyed the reunion and indulged in a mild celebration that night – but we still managed a good early start the next morning. One bloke who thought his day had got off to a really *great* start was the cab driver who we summoned to ferry us from our hotel back to the spot where I'd stopped walking the previous day. Quite understandably, he was keen to know where we were going. In his excitement and eagerness to get on the road, Peter took his question in the broad context of the overall walk and told him we were headed for John O'Groats. For a few seconds the driver thought he had the fare of a lifetime before we disabused him and gave him details of our more modest, immediate, local destination.

It was great to have Peter along. He was clearly quite excited at the prospect of the walk and vented his enthusiasm emphatically and at very frequent intervals. I just hoped he felt equally enthusiastic come four o'clock that afternoon. But there were, admittedly, substantial grounds for optimism. We had a map. We had a reasonably clear idea where we wanted to go. We had accommodation in Glasgow booked for the night and it was a gloriously sunny morning. Crucially, I also had my new pair of boots. We walked cheerfully down the path into the Chatelherault Country Park.

Within a few minutes we were lost. So profoundly lost, in fact, that I was giving my Wannabe Explorer compass its first outing since Bodmin Moor. I'd suggested using the park because it represented a pleasant alternative to walking the 2 miles along the road to the outskirts of Hamilton. Just a brief and gentle loosener in rural surroundings – a way of avoiding a lungful or two of traffic fumes before we very soon got down to the serious urban business of the day. We shambled around for ages before we had the good fortune to meet John, a fireman on his day off, who showed us the right path and fed the NSPCC tin for good measure. He also, interestingly, suggested fire stations as potential sources of emergency accommodation in the more remote parts of Scotland.

We stuck to the path for a while and arrived at the hunting lodge. Chatelherault was formerly part of the estate of the Duke of Hamilton and had once boasted a palace. This had been demolished but the hunting lodge survives. It was very impressive. If this was just the lodge, goodness knows how big the palace must have been.

Peter and I forged on complacently, only to very soon discover that we were lost again. We crashed around through woods, crossed and re-crossed the River Avon (yes, another one), stopped, started again and retraced our steps. At one juncture I confided to my Dictaphone that I was 'sure we'll find our way out of here at some stage during the day'. Throughout this debacle Peter never lost a shred of his enthusiasm. He continued to declaim wildly about how much he was enjoying himself and what a great idea all this had been.

Eventually, we spotted rooftops and stumbled out of the park into Barncluith, a small but visibly up-market outpost of Hamilton. There then ensued a further lengthy delay while we helped a cyclist make running repairs to his bike. I thought the cyclist might possibly, as a result, become the NSPCC's second donor of the morning, but our sole reward was the information, almost gleefully conveyed, that we were 'miles off course'.

Peter was amazing. The day's walk was seriously behind schedule, we were 'miles off course' and he'd just expended a hugely disproportionate amount of precious energy completing the first, very minor, phase of the walk. And yet he was giving voice to his enthusiasm, if anything, even more volubly than before.

We stopped in Hamilton for a long-delayed and well-deserved cup of coffee and to stock up on supplies for lunch. I was able to reassure Peter that, despite our cyclist friend's gloomy assertion to the contrary, we were headed in roughly the right direction and, encouraged, we carried on north-westwards towards Blantyre.

We hadn't gone far before there was yet another interruption to our progress. But this one was altogether more wholesome and beneficial. We spotted an ice-cream parlour

176

whose sign proclaimed it to be the 'Gold Medal 2004 National Champion for the Best Vanilla Ice Cream in the UK'. It belonged to a Peter Equi & Son. This was too good to miss. The best in the UK. In Hamilton of all places. We crossed the street and went in. Peter wisely didn't bother with the chocolate or the strawberry ice cream; he went straight for the award-winning vanilla. I was slightly concerned because he didn't order an Irn Bru to go with it; I thought that in Scotland, if you weren't accompanying food with scotch, beer or Buckfast fortified wine, it was a statutory requirement to drink Irn Bru. Not so, said Peter. Given the industrial quantities of Irn Bru that Equi kept in his fridge I wasn't convinced but thought it prudent to keep my mouth shut.

Then I realized that there was much more to the shop than I'd first thought. It wasn't really an ice-cream shop at all. The ice cream was a mere sideline. It was actually a chip shop and it was doing a roaring lunchtime trade. It had a rich and varied menu, every item of which had been specifically endorsed by the Scottish Cholesterol Marketing Board. I forgot to check if there were fried Mars bars on the list but would be very surprised if they'd been omitted.

Having been awakened to Hamilton's gastronomic potential, it very soon came home to us that the place was a gourmet's paradise. The baker's shop where we'd stopped to buy our lunch supplies boasted a wonderful choice of sticky buns and cream cakes. We'd then progressed to Peter Equi's noble establishment and now here was a corner shop doing ghee-soaked Indian snacks (the samosas looked delicious). When we reached Blantyre we saw droves of schoolkids disappearing into another large and distinguished-looking chip shop, this one doubling as a pizza parlour. All this impelled Peter to ever more fulsome eulogies of the walk's merits and the enjoyment it was providing.

We'd lost so much time as to render a visit to the David

Livingstone museum in Blantyre out of the question, so we turned north and headed for Uddingston.

Lunch was very much in keeping with the shambolic tenor of the day. We were desperate for a place to sit down. Anything would have done – a bus shelter would have been more than adequate – but all we could find was a wall beside what looked suspiciously like an open sewer. A forensic examination might have revealed minute traces of lettuce in the sandwiches but otherwise they were fine – excellent exemplars of the cholesterol-rich cuisine that had been such a steady and rewarding theme of the morning.

After lunch we walked through Newton and Westburn and then picked up a cycle track that brought us to the River Clyde. Having been exclusively urban ever since our escape from the Chatelherault Country Park, our route now, paradoxically, took on an increasingly rural dimension as we approached the city along the river bank. There was hardly a soul around and, apart from a glimpse of the odd tower block, and a detour round the Hoover factory, there was nothing to tell us we were approaching the heart of a major conurbation.

It was pleasant and peaceful walking along the Clyde but I could sense that Peter was beginning to tire. He was as talkative and as high-spirited as ever but my desperately inept navigation in the Country Park had wasted a lot of energy. The Clyde was becoming increasingly sinuous so it made sense to cut up on to London Road, which offered us straight line access westwards into the city centre. The path from the river emerged on to the main road very close to Parkhead, the home of Glasgow Celtic Football Club. The Lions of Lisbon and Jock Stein stands towered above us. They seemed by far the largest, most modern and best-maintained structures in the neighbourhood.

The East End of Glasgow is an area which, putting it kindly, is in a state of transition. By the mid-70s, following

178

the decline of Glasgow's heavy industries, the East End was one of the most deprived inner city areas in Western Europe. A population of 150,000 in 1951 had fallen to 45,000 a quarter of a century later. A recovery is now in hand. The population has climbed back to around 100,000. We walked past new houses and new business premises but also plenty of empty spaces. There is still much obvious neglect. We called at a store that had not seen a paint brush in several decades, and the New Monaco Bar, with its broken neon signs and heavily graffitied iron grilles, would not have been my top choice of venue to watch the following day's football match.

It didn't take us long to walk down London Road. My attention was partly absorbed by a call from Maureen to let me know that she and Roy had reached Fort William, but it seemed that the walk had come to a gratifyingly quiet and comfortable end when we pitched up in George Square at around 5 p.m.

Wrong again. The walk hadn't come to a quiet and comfortable end at all. Peter had other ideas. I'd suggested that he'd done his job for the day and, having provided excellent support on every conceivable front, he could now retire with honour and take the tube or bus to our hotel in Kelvinside. I could follow on foot in my own time. In any event I wanted to visit the Tourist Office.

Peter wasn't having any of it. Far from drifting to a sedate conclusion, the day was about to change gear and enter a new, unexpected and decidedly manic phase. The first thing we had to do was to go and see Peter's brother. Gilbert is a hot-shot lawyer with a very smart office in West Regent Street. He was in the middle of an important business meeting when we dropped in, but responded in an extremely gracious manner to the two malodorous vagrants who'd suddenly taken over his foyer. Having been given all of 90 seconds notice of our arrival he couldn't completely abandon his work commitments but he was hospitality personified.

He'd also researched for us a route north out of the city for the following day.

When we finally left Gilbert's office I thought that now, finally, was Peter's chance to rest. He'd had a 400-mile drive, an evening that, while not plumbing the outer limits of Bacchanalia, could in no way be described as light, and now a 10-hour day on the road with a rich diet of cholesterol. *I* was tired – and I had the benefit of eight weeks' walking behind me. Peter had every right to be exhausted.

'But no,' he said, 'I've got second wind.'

In the light of what was to follow I should have recognized the warning signs.

From Gilbert's office to our hotel in Kelvinside was still a good two miles' walk up through the West End of Glasgow and past the university. Peter's second wind had translated itself into a non-stop stream of ebullient chatter. It didn't take me long to realize that Peter was revisiting his early manhood. His early working life had been spent in the West End of Glasgow, and every street corner, every bar we passed revived long-buried memories of youthful revelry, sparked sudden joyful reminders of ancient junketing, vivid recollections of a carefree lifestyle long since consigned to the dustbin of history. This wasn't memory lane, this was memory eight-lane superhighway. For Peter this was the absolute highlight of the day – possibly the real reason for making the trip. The reminiscences were unstoppable.

By allowing Peter to carry on and by failing to insist that he climbed directly into a taxi outside Gilbert's office, I'd not only courted disaster, I'd taken it out to dinner and then invited it home to view my etchings. We arrived at our hotel at 7.15 p.m. after a 20-mile day. Peter was grey with exhaustion.

I suggested we freshen up and then reconvene for the most well-deserved beer in twenty-first century history. When he didn't appear at the appointed time I tapped on his door and went in. The curtains were drawn and the bed was occupied. Peter was clearly not a well man.

He'd apparently been overcome by a violent and sustained bout of shivering as soon as he'd arrived in his room. He'd gone very cold but was now keeping warm and intended to go to sleep. He rejected outright the merest suggestion of calling a doctor or of any further assistance, medical or otherwise. He was absolutely fine, he said. No worries. And then he started on again about what a wonderful day it had been and what a great time he was having. The man was insane.

Distraught, I went for a dismal and distracted meal at a Chinese restaurant. I had a restless and broken night's sleep, punctuated with rehearsals of conversations with Pilar, Peter's lovely Spanish wife.

Me: 'Hi Pilar, I just thought I ought to let you know that ... '

Pilar: 'Steve! How are you? How did the walk go?'

Me: 'OK, Pilar, apart from the fact that Peter ... '

Pilar: 'How was the weather?'

Me: 'The weather was fine but ... '

Pilar: 'How did Peter get on?'

Me: 'Ah! Well, Pilar, now that's the point really. I thought I'd better give you this hospital phone number ... '

It was just too horrendous to contemplate.

To my unmitigated, heartfelt relief Peter was fine next morning – all smiles and apologizing profusely for causing concern. Fatigue had obviously got the better of him – either that or nervous exhaustion brought on by an overload of colourful nostalgia.

Our hotel was perfectly positioned to eject us straight on to the Kelvin Walkway, a gentle 8-mile walk out of the city northwards to Milngavie. We'd planned a very easy day, first, to allow a modicum of recovery after the rigours of the previous day but, second, because we needed to get to a bar and watch the football. It was the second game of England's

181

World Cup campaign. Trinidad the opposition and a chance for the team and its manager to redeem themselves after Saturday's flabby and toothless 1–0 victory over Paraguay. After the game we'd go our separate ways and Peter would return to real life in Norwich, contemplating a job well done.

The first leg of the Kelvin Walkway runs for a good distance below street level along the towpath of the River Kelvin. As on the Clyde the previous day, there were few indications that one was in the middle of a metropolis. We strolled up through Maryhill Park, where we had excellent views of the higher ground to the north, rejoined the River Kelvin for a spell and then switched allegiance to its tributary, Allander Water, which brought us into Milngavie in time for lunch.

Cause for mild celebration, especially in view of Peter's recovery and his completion of a testing 28-mile trans-Glasgow yomp.

During the walk up from George Square to Gilbert's office the previous day I'd spotted a bar on Renfield Street that looked sufficiently large and anonymous to be the perfect England-watching location. It had to be large and anonymous because England would, in all probability, play so appallingly badly that the embarrassment quotient for watching Englishmen would be high – intolerably so in a pub that was small and intimate. I'd become alarmed at stories of how the Scots had become a nation of Trinidad supporters and had visions of a bar full of aggressive, jeering locals, all sporting replica Trinidad shirts, howling with derision at English ineptitude and giving any English supporters present a bruisingly hard time. I had Peter with me as a kind of native minder, but it still made sense to choose a big soulless place where one's torment might pass unnoticed.

Peter and I caught the train back into Glasgow from Milngavie and duly returned to the bar on Renfield Street. For the second time that day I felt overwhelming relief. The bar was empty. Peter and I had the place virtually to ourselves. Which was just as well because, although England scraped a victory, they duly played like a bunch of Albanian goatherds. They stirred *me* to a state of anguished derision so only God knows how a roomful of Scots would have reacted.

So Peter's odyssey ended on a rather downbeat note. He'd been terrific company and, thank God, had come through the experience unscathed. *My* odyssey continued. I calculated I now had 808 miles under my belt since Land's End. The next stage was a week in the remote mountain fastness of the West Highland Way. Once again, however, I was going to have company.

11

The West Highland Way winds northwards from Milngavie up the eastern side of Loch Lomond before heading off into some of the wildest terrain in the British Isles. The first day on the Way, from Milngavie to Drymen, is an easy lowland stretch and Neil and I walked the 12 miles in a comfortable four-and-a-half hours, including a stop for lunch. Neil lives in the village of Lochwinnoch, in Renfrewshire, some 15 miles south-west of Glasgow. Like Peter, he'd known about my Lands End–John O'Groats plan more or less since its conception, and, like Peter, he'd insisted from the start that he was going to be part of the action.

I'd emerged from the Renfield Street bar gnashing my teeth and seething with frustration at the flaccid ineptitude of Sven and his team. I'd taken the train to Lochwinnoch and Neil had helped me through the worst of the gnashing and seething. We'd driven up to Milngavie on the morning of Friday 16 June to the start of the West Highland Way.

My first day with Peter had had an interesting dietary dimension and the walk to Drymen with Neil was similarly blessed. Neil had put himself in charge of the lunch menu and, with his inspired collusion, the standards of on-trail cuisine now reached new and dizzying heights. We paused for lunch at the hamlet of Gartness and Neil produced a meal consisting of 6 (six) pork pies. Each. Oh, and a Mars bar. The Scottish Cholesterol Marketing Board should have sent a film crew along to record this epic. In case you're wondering about the pork pies, they were called Mini-Meltons. They tasted wonderful – a peppery bouquet and a long, lingering finish.

We had some time to kill in Drymen before the departure of our bus back to Milngavie and after I'd been to the library and imparted the great news about the pork pies to my blog, Neil reminded me that in the next couple of days I'd be moving into highland midge territory. This wee beastie has a fearsome reputation for spoiling the enjoyment of anyone trying to sample the delights of the great outdoors in Western Scotland. There are a large number of different midge species in Scotland but *Culicoides Impunctatus* (the Highland or Scottish midge) is the one with the bite. The midge is barely visible – its wingspan is only 1.4 millimetres but it can detect a potential food source at a range of 100 metres. Having done this it sends out a chemical signal which calls for reinforcements and the feeding frenzy then begins. Interestingly, it's only the females that bite.

Being mid-June the midge season was upon us and I was quite willing to listen to the local pundits and their dire warnings about the midges. Neil is an experienced walker and someone whose opinion I trust on all manner of subjects, so we duly went looking for midge repellant. We exchanged views with the lady at the post office on the merits and demerits of various potions – and, in particular, bog myrtle, which was her establishment's midge repellant of choice. But I wasn't looking for bog myrtle – I was looking for a substance that wasn't designed as a repellant at all but that, for some strange reason, has now acquired a mythical reputation as the wonder-weapon in mankind's epic struggle against the 1.4 millimetre foe.

It's probably an apocryphal story but during the filming of the Mel Gibson epic *Braveheart*, somebody noticed that those members of the team wearing the ordinary skin cosmetic

'Avon So Soft' were not being troubled by the midges. And thus the legend was born. Avon's sales in Scotland must have rocketed. Normally their products are only available via mail order but we found a shop in Drymen that had shelves which were groaning with the stuff.

Job done – so, it being afternoon teatime, I entrusted myself once more to Neil's infinitely superior knowledge and wisdom on the dietary front. Neil introduced me to something called a 'bride's piece', a cake of exceptional richness and heaviness. It was excellent, and I would imagine it occupies a prime spot in any book of recipes produced or endorsed by the Scottish Cholesterol Marketing Board.

That evening we repaired to The Brown Bull in Lochwinnoch where I continued the research into Scottish beer. The Harviestoun (brewed in Clackmannanshire) went down well. I was also interested to see how The Brown Bull had dealt with the ban on smoking in public places, which had come into effect nearly three months earlier. The simple act of drawing breath was now a pleasure in the main bar, where previously the air quality had been roughly on a par with that of the great London smog of 1952 which killed 4,000 people. Smokers were now accommodated in a kind of impromptu shelter at the back of the pub among a disparate collection of old armchairs, and this had now become a social focus in its own right and an integral part of the The Brown Bull 'experience'. Neil has a wide circle of family and friends among the patrons of The Brown Bull and their generosity towards the NSPCC that evening was quite exceptional.

Work commitments prevented Neil from joining me on day two of the West Highland Way but he kindly drove me back to Drymen for the start of the day's walk northwards to Rowardennan. It was another easy enough day up the east side of Loch Lomond but the weather was drizzly and overcast and the greyness and generally poor visibility gave

186

the hills a one-dimensional quality, silhouettes against a dark sky. I noted that the forecast for the next few days was similarly bleak.

I bypassed Conic Hill, the only elevation of any note on this section of the trail, and trudged along the side of the loch, mainly in woodland, to Rowardennan, a small settlement which sits in the shadow of Ben Lomond about halfway up the loch. My B&B there was run by a lady called Lucy Fraser, a regular participant in charity endurance events. She was planning to take part in a 70-miles-in-24-hours event a few weeks after my visit, and I was duly impressed. Not half as impressed as I was, however, when I asked her about her children. She'd been talking about her sons (plural) and daughters (plural) and the plurals prompted me to ask how many children she actually had. 'Eight' was the response. And I thought *I'd* had a busy life.

It was wet when I set out on Sunday 18 June and the rain didn't let up for most of the day. As a result visibility was poor on some parts of the path under the conifers and I was startled as a dark shape seemed to suddenly detach itself from a tree just ahead and move towards me. An unusual place for a mugging I thought, before realizing it was Neil. He'd driven up to the hotel at Inversnaid that morning and had walked back to meet me. It had all been planned but I hadn't expected him this early. We walked on up the loch to the hotel. It's a magnificent building both inside and out. The panelled lounge where we ate our lunch was empty but deserved to be full of kilts and tweed suits, while the view of the loch on a decent day would have been stunning. Very atmospheric, although the 'foreign' accents of the splendid Mancunian who served us lunch, and his legions of Polish helpers, didn't quite gel with the ambience.

Loch Lomond narrows as it progresses northwards, becomes more fjord-like, with steeper sides, and after lunch the going became significantly tougher. I didn't read Andrew

McCloy's description of this section until later – but let him take up the story.

The last few miles of lochside from Inversnaid are arduous (*masterly understatement*). There is little in the way of a path; rather a jumble of boulders and tree roots (*yes*). It can be particularly hazardous in wet weather when the rocks are slippery (*like now, you mean?*) and especially dangerous for those carrying large packs (*thanks, Andrew, masterly understatement*).

It really was very unpleasant, up to then at least, the most difficult stretch of the entire walk. Because of the steepness of the lochside a tumble on the slippery rocks could have had very nasty consequences. I was very pleased that Neil was there to monitor progress and to give occasional help with the rucksack.

Neil stayed with me until the path eased – much later than he had intended, although I'm sure he would never admit it. We then said goodbye – but only for the moment because he was planning to spend another weekend on the road with me some 14 days hence during the final push towards John O'Groats. Whereas he'd managed this current phase of the walk from home, his next involvement would involve a 600-mile round trip. And he wouldn't be getting a scenic lochside walk for all his trouble either. This would be a 600-mile round trip for the privilege of spending two days walking along the A9. What with Peter's antics and now this, I seemed to be surrounded by a coterie of Scottish lunatics.

It was still raining when I arrived at my destination for the night. This was Inverarnan, right at the top of Loch Lomond, where I'd booked a room at The Drovers Inn, an apparently well-known hotel beside the main A82 highway. My preference was still to avoid hotels, wherever possible, in favour of B&Bs on grounds of both price and quality, but the £30 I'd been quoted for bed and breakfast at The Drovers didn't seem outrageous. It was certainly a more appealing prospect than the campsite. I was wet and tired when I arrived and hardly took in any of the surroundings as I checked in and went to my room.

It was when I got to the room that I switched on again and started to take note of what was happening. Although it was still early, it was a dark evening and the volume of light entering the room through the small and grimy window was minuscule. I looked around for the light switch – and was still looking about 15 minutes later. I looked everywhere. Inside the room, outside the room, high up on the wall, low down, over the bed – any location that could conceivably harbour a light switch. I was utterly baffled. In my tiredness and discomfort strange thoughts started to invade my mind. *Was* there a light switch? After all, the place did look rather primitive. Or was this some kind of *Candid Camera* stunt designed to lure the unwary occupant into making a complete clown of himself as he searched, doing and saying all kinds of humiliating things in front of a hidden audience of millions.

Remembering the embarrassing incident at Land's End when I'd had to return to the front desk for further directions, I was hesitant to seek assistance from a member of the hotel staff. The ones I'd seen were all about 12 years old and a conversation with any of them that began, 'Excuse me but could you help me find a light switch?' was bound to lead to further indignity and ridicule. Nevertheless, I was just about to admit defeat when I found it. The switch was set in the door frame. Both frame and switch were both painted the same sepulchral black colour and the only way of finding the switch was the way I'd just followed – a chance brush of the hand over the relevant area.

Actually, when I turned the light on it made very little difference. There was a 5 watt bulb in the light fitting and the room was still filled with Stygian gloom. I could barely see to

189

unpack the rucksack. And when I did, the only place to put stuff was on a couple of wire hangers that hung on the back of the door.

I was on my guard now and took much more notice of my environment when I eventually went downstairs again. Down in the lobby there was a collection of dusty old cabinets full of stuffed animals, including a striking but rather moth-eaten old bear. Outside, the brickwork and windows were, in estate agent parlance 'in need of a little attention', and inside, the wallpaper and the electrics had clearly remained unchanged since the hotel's construction in 1705. I thought wistfully of the tasteful furnishings and punctilious service that were hallmarks of Lucy Fraser's establishment at Rowardennan.

I missed the best bit of The Drovers. The bar had a real fire going and would have been much more hospitable than the mundane pub across the road, which lured me in with the prospect of big-screen World Cup football. A shame. I also decided to give the cooked breakfast option a miss, having seen an exemplar arrive at a neighbouring table and felt my enthusiasm wane rapidly. This was the authentic 'full Scottish breakfast'. I'm unsure of the chef's nationality but I'm prepared to make a handsome wager that he wasn't Scottish. His front-of-house colleagues, although all sporting kilts and sporrans, were of largely Antipodean origin. I didn't encounter a single Scottish member of staff during my entire sojourn at The Drovers.

Am I being critical of The Drovers? Well, in a way I suppose I am. But would I want it to change? Not necessarily. The occasional light dusting wouldn't come amiss, but it's far better (and far more memorable) in its current state than it would be if it was renovated and re-packaged as some trite and tasteless tourist trap. Guide books describe it (accurately) as 'idiosyncratic' and 'resolutely old-fashioned' and it should strive to retain these characteristics. After all, the place has a long history and a genuine cult following. You

190

can even buy 'Drovers Inn' T-shirts. I almost bought one. Almost.

The gloom persisted the next day, although the rain was only intermittent. It was a 12-mile stint from Inverarnan to Tyndrum up the valley of the River Falloch, skirting Crianlarich to the west and then heading north-west by the River Fillan. Much of the route was over an eighteenth-century military road, and from here on the West Highland Way makes extensive use of the work of the Redcoat soldiers of General Wade and Major Caulfield. It was King George I who dispatched General Wade to the Highlands in 1724 to reconnoitre the place and, in particular, to review the effectiveness of the military response to the constant threat of insurgency among the unruly clans. General Wade's report emphasized the difficulties the local military commanders were experiencing as a result of the severe shortage of roads and bridges. He was duly sent back to the Highlands to rectify the situation, and by the time of his promotion to Field Marshal in 1740 he had overseen the building of some 300 miles of military road. Over the next 25 years, his successor, Major Caulfield, added substantially to this tally. Much of the work is, of course, still evident today. I wondered what the Redcoats made of it all – the weather, the marauding clans and the patchy quality of accommodation at places like The Drovers.

Tyndrum is a tiny place on the main road up to Fort William. It owes its livelihood almost exclusively to tourism, a fact evidenced by an establishment I visited on my arrival. Its amalgam of restaurants, outdoor supply shops, supermarket, whiskey store and souvenir emporium makes the duty free at Heathrow Airport look like a struggling corner shop. Tyndrum is the smallest settlement in the United Kingdom to boast two railway stations. Not only that, two actual railway lines as well. The line forks at Crianlarich but the two sets of tracks then run up to Tyndrum, one on each bank of the Fillan, before going their separate ways – one to Oban and the other to Fort William. I also passed a loch where Robert the Bruce is reputed to have thrown away his weapons after a military setback against the MacDougall clan in 1306, and the site of a former lead crushing plant, where the ground was still completely barren despite the fact that the facility closed over 100 years ago.

The other place I visited was Paddy's Bar, which was an exceptionally friendly pub, but I made a mistake there which showed just how far I still had to go with my Scottish beer research project. Encouraged by the modest but reasonable quality of the McEwans 80 Shilling I'd tasted in Moffat, I assumed that its Tennents namesake would be equally palatable. Bad call. I was back in liquid cardboard territory again. Tennents 80 Shilling was a very ordinary beer. I'd found out that this strange 'Shilling' designation was a reference to the amount of duty that was payable, long ago of course, on a barrel of the stuff, but I'd also somehow assumed that the higher the number of shillings in a name, the higher the quality of the product. The Tennents experiment tended to disprove this theory. More work was required.

Day five on the West Highland Way started innocuously enough. It was Tuesday 20 June and although still very overcast, the weather was at least dry. The B&B in Tyndrum had a magnificent drying room and I'd celebrated by undertaking a real purge on the laundry front. For the first time in many days I felt clean and fresh as I walked along the old military road north out of Tyndrum. I'd lost one railway line (it had headed west out of Tyndrum towards Oban) but the other was still there. In order to maintain height it describes a wonderful loop around the sides of a couple of mountains and crosses a viaduct before continuing its route to Bridge Of Orchy. This was well worth keeping an eye on, as was the shepherd that I could see in the distance high up to my right on the mountainside as the clouds started to lift. He was whistling to his dog, which was some way below him trying to collect a few recalcitrant sheep. The acoustics were such that the shepherd's whistling reverberated all over the valley. The dog scampered around, cornered the sheep and then crouched alertly in front of them.

By the time I reached Bridge of Orchy the weather had definitely started to improve and, for the very first time on the West Highland Way, I no longer had to take the guide book on trust when it spoke about the excellent looming job being performed by the mountains. I liked Bridge of Orchy, the bridge itself being a beautifully proportioned stone construction dating from around 1750. A Major Caulfield special.

Leaving Bridge Of Orchy the trail climbs through pine forest and then crests the rise of Mam Carraigh, a hill, which, by Highland standards, is exceptionally modest. But despite the low elevation, the view was magnificent. The landscape was bathed in sunshine and now, finally, on the fifth day of the West Highland Way I had something to look at. I could see north and west over Loch Tulla and the wilderness of Rannoch Moor that I was due to cross that afternoon. There were authentic mountain peaks all around. It was superb.

I walked down the hill feeling relaxed and optimistic. At last the gloom that had been the keynote of the weather ever since Milngavie appeared to have lifted. At the bottom of the hill I stopped at the Inveroran Hotel for a well-deserved late morning coffee. I threw my rucksack down and addressed a few cheery celebratory remarks at a group occupying an outside table. Without realizing it I'd gatecrashed the staff's morning break but I was soon forgiven and I started to comment enthusiastically on the sudden improvement in the weather.

'Ah, but there's heavy rain forecast,' said a member of the team. 'If you're crossing Rannoch Moor I wouldn't hang around.'

I hadn't bothered to check the forecast that morning. But, if true, this was dire news. Because the next stage of the walk was perhaps the bleakest, most isolated section of the whole end-to-end walk.

After a quick coffee I took the advice of the Inveroran hotel team and hurried on. A brief look at the guidebook imparted the encouraging news that the Moor 'needs to be treated with respect, for there is no shelter and no escape from whatever the weather chooses to throw at the walker'.

It's around 9 miles from Forest Lodge at the western end of Loch Tulla to the Kingshouse Hotel at the eastern end of Glencoe. The intervening stretch of bleak moorland is Rannoch Moor. Unlike its counterpart at Bodmin, several hundred miles to the south, the moor has a good path which takes a more or less direct course at an altitude of between 550 and 1,100 feet. A sign at its beginning proclaims it to be one of Thomas Telford's Parliamentary roads, the great engineer having been commissioned in 1803 to build new roads and bridges in the Highlands, mainly as a result of the military roads beginning to fall into disrepair and being unable to cope with the increasing demands of commercial traffic.

The path made a fairly undramatic start from Forest Lodge, climbing gently with a large pine plantation on one side. It was only when the trees gave out that the true nature of the moor began to assert itself. It's a wilderness of peat, rough grass and heather. It's very wet, with pools and bogs at every turn. Just a few bare stumps of old trees and high, dark mountains in every direction.

I walked for a while with Tom and Marie, who'd been camping until their tent had given up the ghost the previous night at Bridge of Orchy. I shuddered to think what their 'holiday' had been like under canvas. They pressed on while I ate lunch, taking advantage of the minimal shelter afforded by what my map told me was the last clump of conifers before Kingshouse. The sun had disappeared and the gloom had returned. As I ate I glanced back the way I had come. There to the south was an absolutely monumental wall of weather. As I started off again the first drops of rain began to fall.

To start with it wasn't that unpleasant. The rain was bearable and, importantly, the rapidly strengthening wind was blowing from behind. But then the rain got harder, a lot harder. The wind increased to gale force and all I could see was the shifting, eddying clouds and mist and the occasional dark, one-dimensional mountain hulk.

I honestly think that if the wind had been blowing from in front I might not have made it. Within a very few minutes my 'waterproof' trousers were completely overwhelmed. They were actually the old overtrousers that my son had used for skiing and they'd been perfectly adequate for the constant drizzle in Staffordshire and the odd shower in Cornwall. Now, however, my legs were saturated and my boots, in turn, rapidly became waterlogged. I could feel them getting heavier by the minute. It wasn't a cold day but the sodden clothing was making me *feel* cold.

It was very odd, but in a way quite atmospherically appropriate, that in this howling Wagnerian twilight I got the saddest phone call of the entire walk. When the mobile rang my first reaction was one of amazement that there was a signal in this God-forsaken place. But the call put my own current privations into perspective. It was from Geoff, not the purveyor of shirts but another friend and former work colleague. He told me that an old mutual business friend had died suddenly. What was really sad, though, was the fact that this guy had been trying to retire for ages and, well into his seventies, had eventually, at long last succeeded. He'd suffered a fatal heart attack a matter of days after he'd finally stopped working.

I slogged on feeling very depressed, as the rain became, if possible, even harder. I wondered what had become of Tom and Marie. My boots felt like lead weights. But after the

195

phone call my discomfort was not seriously prolonged. The wind hurled me along at a terrific pace and at about 3.30 I was able to make out, to my great relief, the headlights of the traffic on the A82. Within 20 minutes I was dripping litres of water onto the carpet of the reception area of the Kingshouse Hotel.

That night I had by far the worst night's sleep of the entire walk. This was not in any way a reflection of the standard of creature comforts provided by the Kingshouse Hotel. Quite the reverse – the tea and hot scones that I was served in front of a blazing fire about an hour after my arrival was one of the highlights of the entire trip. No, what kept me awake for most of the night was the wind.

I'd had an interesting evening watching the latest instalment of the England football team's halting progress through the World Cup finals. There was a little sports bar at the back of the hotel and it was there that I'd sat in a thinly populated room and witnessed Sven's boys muddle their way through to a 2–2 draw against Sweden, thereby guaranteeing their progress through to the next stage of the competition. Although it was another embarrassing performance, there wasn't a single Scot present to see it, the sparse, and thankfully very quiet, audience being composed of Dutch, Slovaks and a few morose Scandinavians sunk in Ibsenesque gloom.

When I left the bar it was still daylight, although the clouds remained very low. The rain had stopped but the wind was now utterly ferocious. It howled and screamed and whistled around the hotel. It wasn't a constant or a symmetrical wind. It would slow quite markedly for a few moments before a fresh gust would slam into the wall of the building with a reverberating thud, rattling the fittings and the window frames. I was rattled too. I lay in bed and read the guidebook, trying to glean some advance intelligence about the next day's walk. The book wasn't really much help. All it could do was tell me what a splendid time I was having and how lucky

I was to be here. What I *should* have been witnessing, apparently, was 'the most exhilarating mountain scenery in Britain', not to mention a 'photographer's dream'. What I'd actually seen was a view that hadn't changed since my arrival – namely the lower slopes of mountains and a sinister, narrow tunnel of cloud, which on a better day would be recognizable as the entrance to Glencoe.

When I eventually put the light out it was like trying to sleep through an artillery barrage. I had a desperately broken and disturbed night, punctuated at one point by a trip to the drying room to see if there had been any improvement to the sorry condition of my waterlogged footwear. There hadn't.

Come morning, the weather was unchanged. I considered staying put for the day, but it was only a 'short' 9 mile stretch to Kinlochleven and the other hardy souls in the hotel seemed to be preparing themselves for action. I girded my loins, put on my damp boots and was ready to go before 9 o'clock. The weather forecast was 'blustery' – probably in the same way that Hurricane Katrina had been blustery. It was 21 June – Midsummer's Day.

I stuck my nose out of the door and very soon discovered that the wind was now 'blustering' in a new and unexpected direction. As I headed west from Kingshouse down into Glencoe the wind was now in my face. It seemed to have done a brisk about-turn since the previous afternoon. I struggled along, virtually bent double, my morale not improved by the fact that, while this was bad enough, my next hurdle was something cosily and amiably entitled 'The Devil's Staircase'.

I found it some 3 miles along the flat from Kingshouse where the West Highland Way turns north and makes what, surprisingly, is its first really seriously rugged climb since leaving Milngavie. The Devil's Staircase is another section of old military road that zig-zags its way up the hillside for about 850 feet. It actually wasn't too bad. Given the conditions, of course, I could see virtually nothing of the 'exhilarating mountain scenery' but I was more than content that by some fluke configuration of the mountain contours I was now relatively sheltered from the wind. And, magically, it hadn't actually rained yet either.

By the time I'd reached the top of The Devil's Staircase and started the descent I was perhaps halfway to Kinlochleven. Things had gone much better so far than I'd feared during the more sombre periods of my night-time vigil. But as the slow descent began it started to rain again. Very soon the wind was back with a vengeance and this time it was right in my face.

After a while I tried to pretend that water was my natural element. The path, completely overwhelmed by the accumulation of rainfall, was now a shallow, fast-flowing stream. From the waist down I was so wet that I might, indeed, have passed for a fish. My boots weighed a ton. It was an action replay of Rannoch Moor, only worse. I guess there was *one* consolation. It was far too wet and windy for midges.

It wasn't life threatening but it was by far the most unpleasant piece of walking I've ever had to endure. Teeth were duly gritted, fists were clenched, and I struggled down the mountain to Kinlochleven. I arrived just after one o'clock and for the second time in 24 hours went and dripped copiously and unsociably on somebody's floor. This time it was the turn of the Ice Rock Shop, so called because it has an ice wall where people can practice their climbing. I watched this for a spell while I lunched, and then repaired to the actual shop where I bought a pair of proper waterproof trousers and some gaiters to divert the downward flow of water away from my boots. A sure guarantee, I thought, that it wouldn't rain again before John O'Groats.

I was in a low and chastened frame of mind. It occurred to me that I'd actually become rather complacent about the end-to-end walk. I'd thoroughly enjoyed the Lake District, airily dismissed Southern Scotland as boring and then just had a rollicking good time walking with Peter and Neil. The deities that ordain these things had clearly decided that I was no longer taking things seriously enough and thought it was time to teach me a lesson. I'd covered 885 miles and it would be regrettable, to say the least, if I was deflected from my objective at this late stage. The blog entry I recorded at Kinlochleven library is a veritable flood of eloquence compared to most of its predecessors. It seems to recognize the need for persistence. 'Never mind,' it says, 'bash on.'

I received immediate help in my 'bashing' endeavours from Danny Sweeney. I was lucky that in Kinlochleven, by pure chance, I'd chosen the B&B run by the western world's leading expert in getting things dry. Danny took my wet gear and by some mysterious alchemy had everything completely dry by the next morning. How he achieved this feat on my boots I shall never know. Actually, for all I do know, he probably does it every week. It turned out that Roy and Maureen had stayed with him a few days previously.

Kinlochleven used to be a company town, but in 2000 Alcan closed its aluminium smelter, almost a century after the town's first aluminium plant had started operations. To recover from the setback Kinlochleven was trying to switch its commercial focus to tourism and to foster the growth of smaller enterprises. One of these is the Atlas Brewery, and it was disappointing that its (apparently excellent) product was not available at the Tailrace Inn, the pub I visited that evening. Instead I had to settle for some more mediocre 80 Shilling keg stuff. Another setback to the research project.

As Danny and I chatted over breakfast next morning the weather was overcast but dry. However, the forecast was 'showery' and, given the understated nature of Scottish weather forecasts, I was not hopeful. 'Showery' in local parlance probably equated to the description of 'blustery' that had been attached to yesterday's hurricane.

Sure enough, as I set out, it started to rain again.

Kinlochleven sits in a very narrow valley and some parts of the town do not see direct sunlight for several months of the year. Apart from the road by the side of the loch, any way out of the town is therefore bound to be steep. The West Highland Way climbs sharply, heading north-westwards out of the town through the woods. It was heavy going in the wet and I anticipated a long and difficult day ahead – 14 miles to Fort William.

But as I crested the top of the hill the rain had eased and I even had the pleasure of a view. It was back over Kinlochleven and the steep-sided bowl in which it lay. I could see the huge water pipes that used to feed the aluminium works running in parallel down the opposite hillside and the narrow finger of Loch Leven stretching away to the west. It was a good omen.

And the rest of the day was OK. Although it remained overcast it also remained dry, and as I approached Fort William the clouds parted to allow me a fleeting glimpse of the lower slopes of Ben Nevis. The last mile or so of the West Highland Way into the town is along the road, a somewhat prosaic and anti-climactic finale to seven days of toil and tears. I passed the Wishing Stone, a large chunk of rock which local legend endows with magical properties, and was lucky enough to witness a bride, in full white wedding regalia, jump out of a car and make her own private oblation before it. As I passed she grinned at me sheepishly before returning to her car and driving away.

I felt a real sense of achievement when I got to Fort William and the end of the West Highland Way. Seven days and 90-odd miles, nearly every one of which I'd had to hack out of granite. Given the time of year the conditions had been extreme. I also felt I'd got over the last major barrier of the walk. I reckoned I now only had another 11 days' walking over relatively easy terrain. Four days through the Great Glen to Inverness and from there a week to the finishing line.

The weather forecast was a lot better too. All this made me feel good. After days in the outback it was also 'sheep shearer hits town' syndrome again and I was therefore going to celebrate with a curry. This made me feel even better. And when I explained my tribulations on the trail to Mrs Egan, my B&B landlady, and she said 'Oh, you are hard,' my cup of joy overflowed completely.

12

My four days in the Great Glen seemed like a period of gentle convalescence after all the trauma and sensory deprivation of the West Highland Way. The weather was dry and calm and the terrain generally undemanding. Geologically speaking, the Great Glen is a tear-fault and, according to Andrew McCloy, the most active earthquake zone in Britain. It runs dead straight for around 70 miles north-eastwards from Fort William to Inverness.

The Great Glen is navigable by water for its entire length. Three lochs (Loch Lochy, Loch Oich and Loch Ness) and 22 miles of man-made waterway collectively form the Caledonian Canal – and having had so much assistance from canals ever since Somerset, it was fitting that this monster should give the walk its canal finale. It's not quite in the class of the Manchester Ship Canal, but the Caledonian accommodates large sea-going commercial and pleasure vessels and needs no fewer than 29 locks to manage changes in gradient.

It seems that cost overruns, and optimistic assessments of the time required for major projects, are not just a modern phenomenon. The Caledonian Canal was begun in 1803 to plans produced by Thomas Telford, its basic purpose being to provide a quicker, safer alternative to the hazardous sea journey around the north of Scotland. Construction costs were budgeted at £350,000 over the estimated seven-year period required for completion. Nineteen years and £840,000 later, when the canal finally opened, it still wasn't as deep as Telford had originally planned and was too shallow to accommodate many of the increasingly large ships being built at the time. It was only after they'd had another go in the 1840s that the canal finally emerged in the shape that Telford had first intended.

Perhaps unsurprisingly there's a long-distance footpath through the Great Glen. Equally unsurprisingly it's called the Great Glen Way and (if you include the Bollin Valley Way) it was the eighth, and last, long-distance trail of the end-to-end walk. It begins, very prosaically, in the car park of Morrison's supermarket in Fort William, and I hadn't been on the trail for more than 90 seconds when I passed a man who assured me it was a fine day for the midges. After all the nasty weather of the last few days it would have been difficult to find anything remotely negative to say about the conditions that morning, but this guy succeeded. He reminded me of Frazer, the perennially pessimistic old Scottish character in *Dad's Army*. Perhaps, like Frazer, he was the local undertaker.

In fact there'd been an item on Scottish midges on the BBC *Breakfast* TV programme that morning showing people wandering around in the sort of outfit you wear if you're contemplating going out to catch swarms of killer bees. My Avon So Soft still lay unused in my rucksack and I wondered if Frazer knew something that I didn't.

It was the most pleasant walking I'd had in many days – a major relief to be unencumbered with waterproofs. Leaving Fort William I passed Neptune's Staircase, a flight of eight consecutive locks that raises vessels 70 feet over a distance of 500 yards, and made good time along the towpath to Gairlochy. No problems with midges either.

At Gairlochy the canal flows into Loch Lochy and the Way continues above the loch through coniferous forest. It was a pattern that was to become standard over the next few days.

Long, quiet, restful stretches through the woods with occasional views over Loch Lochy or Loch Ness.

I walked the length of Loch Lochy that afternoon and spent the night at the youth hostel at Laggan. This was the first youth hostel of the walk, and the first night I'd spent in one since 1971. There was no pub within reach and no lime curd or organic rhubarb for breakfast, but for £13 it was fine. The hostel was managed with great charm and efficiency by a young German girl – further proof of the Scottish tourist industry's total apparent reliance on foreign adolescents. Where was the youth of Scotland? Were they all away running pubs in Prague or youth hostels in the Bavarian Alps? It was all rather puzzling.

The youth hostel at Laggan wasn't a youth hostel at all. It was a cheap crash for middle-aged Glaswegians on walking weekends, and I didn't feel at all out of place. I ended up sharing a dormitory with three other gentlemen, all of whom were commendably restrained and tidy, and none of whom snored. I did actually wonder whether *I* was the one who snored (after all there's always one isn't there?) but none of my room-mates threw any accusing looks in my direction next morning or looked noticeably wan or hollow-eyed through lack of sleep.

Breakfast at the youth hostel wasn't a great success – which was entirely my own fault as I'd omitted to plan ahead and bring my own supplies. I was therefore restricted to the contents of the hostel's rather meagrely stocked grocery counter but, even then, the cornflakes and Mars bar were more enjoyable and sustaining than Jennifer's poxy takeaway breakfast in Wilmslow. Understandably, however, by the time I'd walked the length of Loch Oich and some more canal to reach Fort Augustus, I was definitely in a mood to enjoy lunch. Which I did. In the sunshine. Sitting by the ladder of locks and watching the world go by. Another moment to savour.

I'd had a wonderful little cameo moment on the stretch of canal into Fort Augustus. I passed a fisherman wearing the first deerstalker hat I'd seen used in a non-theatrical context for a very long time. An hour or so later I saw him again – he'd obviously abandoned his original post and motored to what he hoped would be a more productive spot further up the canal. We recognized each other and, in response to my greeting, he gave vent to a single syllable utterance that packed even more depth and meaning than Leslie Phillips' 'Hello'. It was as if, rather than simply wishing him 'Good morning', I'd said something along the lines of 'Come on, you must finally admit that Scotland will never win the World Cup.' It was a long, quavering, downward glissando. It went on for several seconds and spoke of a reluctant, grudging acceptance of some inescapable but profoundly tragic premise, a sad, final recognition after a lifetime's struggle, of some deeply regrettable but fundamentally unalterable truth.

'Aye,' he said.

I mingled with the tourists in Fort Augustus and then pressed on along the north bank of Loch Ness. I now had a good view of the high mountains behind me to the south-west and the noticeably smaller ones ahead of me. I stopped for the night in Invermoriston and particularly enjoyed my visit to the Glenmoriston Arms, which has more than 150 different types of whisky behind the bar, and was where I sampled the Isle of Skye Brewery's Red Cuillin Ale. It wasn't quite to my taste – a bit too sweet – but, from the meanderings of my research, a basic proposition was just starting to emerge, namely that it *is* possible to get proper beer in Scotland. This theory was amply supported by a brochure I came across at my B&B which contained news of 'real ale' festivals and events around Scotland. I drew enormous comfort from the surprising news that it was possible to get Adnams Broadside in Clachnaharry (wherever that may be).

I was away from Invermoriston early the next morning, Sunday 25 June. There was a degree of urgency about my progress because the England game kicked off at 4.00 p.m. and I wanted to be ensconced in front of the TV in good time. I'd selected my B&B very carefully and made my prospective landlady fully aware of my exacting requirements. I was headed for Drumnadrochit, attracted partly by the wonderful name, but also by its convenient location on the trail before the final pull into Inverness.

It was a gloriously sunny morning. The climb out of Invermoriston was a steep one but I was rewarded with spectacular views back down Loch Ness to Fort Augustus and beyond. I sat on a bench, bathed in sunlight, contemplating this vista, munching my way through a packet of plain chocolate wholemeal digestives and glancing through the *Scottish News of the World*. At that juncture I couldn't think of anything more I wanted out of life. The *Scottish News of the World*, quite naturally, featured a whole compendium of articles talking down England's prospects for that afternoon's game against Ecuador. Given the quality of England's previous displays over the past fortnight, it was difficult to find fault with their logic. The Great Glen Way actually left the Great Glen hereabouts, cutting away from Loch Ness through a more low-rise, agricultural landscape. I arrived in Drumnadrochit at around 2.15 p.m. in plenty of time for the football.

'Well, they've had one or two speculative shots and strung a few passes together.' It wasn't so much what Gary Lineker actually said in his half-time commentary, it was the plaintive tone of quiet desperation in his voice that really summed it all up. Equipped with some of the finest individual players in world football, Sven Goran Eriksson had somehow contrived to coax from his team another performance of such abject quality, such non-existent cohesion, as to beggar the belief of even the most long-suffering and deeply pessimistic English supporter. How could the whole be so much inferior to the sum total of its parts? How was this man Eriksson able to turn so much gold into dross? Here was a team of professionals, earning millions of pounds a year each, who had 'managed to string a few passes together'. Against Ecuador for God's sake! I was very relieved that, for the first time since the Paraguay debacle I'd witnessed in Lockerbie, I was watching an England game alone.

An hour or so into the game David Beckham scored for England, thereby managing to squeak his team through into the quarter finals. My feeling of relief was tempered by the thought that I'd have to go through all this anguish again quite soon. I'd need to check on the date and time of the next game and schedule my walking to accommodate it.

I was the guest of Allan and Sue at their excellent B&B close to the centre of Drumnadrochit. The B&B backed on to the Ben Leven Hotel which provided more ample opportunity to continue the research project. The food was no great shakes but the Harviestoun Ptarmigan was quite palatable. All in all, Drumnadrochit was kind to me. Allan and Sue made an exceptionally generous donation to the NSPCC. I enjoyed the centre of the village, with its green and, as I rejoined the northern shore of Loch Ness the following morning, there were excellent views back to Urquhart Castle. I vowed that next time I'd visit the Official Loch Ness Monster Exhibition Centre.

I was also much taken by the signs at the main car park which exhorted foreign motorists to drive on the left. I just wondered whether those visitors who hadn't absorbed this lesson by the time they hit Drumnadrochit would ever get the hang of it. It was there that I spotted a car with the number plate NES 51E, surely the most valuable registration number in town.

The final leg of the Great Glen Way is the 19-mile stretch between Drumnadrochit and Inverness. Initially, it was a return to the Great Glen and a climb up through the forest but then the path cut north away from the loch up to a height of around 1,200 feet – a good long climb which lasted some two hours, and which was, if I'd worked it all out correctly, the last major climb of the entire end-to-end journey.

I enjoyed the afternoon's walk to Inverness. It gave me a distinct feeling of change, a strong impression of discernible progress. For one thing, the landscape was changing. It was still raw and mountainous to the west, with rough fields and moorland, but it was lower, more open and less grandiose than the Highlands. Down to my left was my first firth, the Beauly Firth, the first of a series encountered by the walker along Scotland's north-east coast. And then, coming to a break in the forest, I was presented with a panoramic view of Inverness spread out before me.

The Great Glen Way takes a rather circuitous path down through the suburbs of Inverness and then rejoins the Caledonian Canal for one last hurrah before the end of the trail. To celebrate my arrival in the city I paused to buy an ice cream at an extraordinary place that could, on reflection, have been the head office of the Scottish Cholesterol Marketing Board. It seemed to combine every possible species of cholesterol under one capacious roof. It was a junk-food theme park, the absolute antithesis of the health food shop or vegetarian restaurant. It was ultra-modern, computerized, spotlessly clean and it was equipped to dispense fish and chips, burgers, ice cream and pizzas in industrial quantities. There were fleets of delivery vans parked outside, poised to transport cholesterol in whatever form that was required to any point in the Highland region at a moment's notice. The Irn Bru was probably delivered by pipeline. We just don't have places like that south of the border.

A little further down the street I was slightly concerned to note that Inverness boasted a 'Victim Support' shop. The city obviously contained so many victims it needed a separate shop to handle them all. Like the cholesterol theme park it was a concept I hadn't come across before. I resolved to take extra care.

As I walked up to my B&B I saw something else in the distance that gave me a degree of concern but I consigned it to the back of my mind. I wanted to make the most of Inverness. I'd imagined a small, somewhat dour place but Inverness came across as quite the reverse. It's obviously a thriving hub with a large and well-stocked retail sector. One strong distinguishing feature was the almost eerie speed of the service in the local Wetherspoon establishment. For the record, the Red Kite ale from the Black Isle Brewery was very palatable.

I went to the library and had a good look around. Inverness looked a sturdy, appealing kind of place and in some ways it would have been good to have stayed longer. But I wasn't awarding myself holidays any more. I seemed to be losing the desire to stand and stare – I'd been on the road for nearly ten weeks now, I'd covered 973 miles and the closer I got to John O'Groats the more intent I was on finishing what I'd started.

The sight that had caused me a frisson of concern as I walked up to Mr and Mrs Hogg's B&B that Monday evening was a bridge. And the next morning, Tuesday 27 June I had to cross it. Not, on the face of it, an insuperable problem. Unless, like me, you suffer from an acute fear of heights. I knew it was going to be tricky and understood, now, the significance of a remark that Maureen had made to me in the course of our last telephone conversation. She'd rung me during my evening at the youth hostel in Laggan to let me know that she and Roy had got as far as Dornoch, about 40 miles north of Inverness. As usual, I'd asked her for tips about the accommodation en route and about other salient features of the walk. She'd made a remark, which I hadn't taken in at the time, about an unpleasant bridge at Inverness.

209

I'd called her remark briefly to mind when, the previous afternoon, I'd arrived at the River Ness suspension bridge. This is a long, narrow footbridge which crosses the river at an insignificant height. It's a poor man's version of the Thames footbridge between St Paul's and the Tate Modern. Like its London counterpart before it was redesigned, the Ness suspension bridge wobbles a bit, but not enough to cause alarm to any but the very, very faintest of hearts. The thought had passed through my mind that if Maureen thought this bridge was nasty, she wasn't the feisty lady I took her for. 'Women', I thought, before dismissing the subject from my mind.

But now, of course, I realised that Maureen hadn't meant the Ness Bridge at all. She'd been talking about the Kessock Bridge, and I could see straightaway that this was very nasty indeed.

The Kessock Bridge was built in 1982. It takes the A9 over the narrow strait between the Beauly and Moray Firths. It's a suspension bridge, 1,150 yards long, a fine structure with clean, attractive lines. It's also very, very high.

Acrophobia, on the other hand, is the medical term for an acute fear of heights. It's a condition that involves a feeling, when at heights, of being pushed or mentally impelled over the edge.

The Kessock Bridge is clearly not a good place for people with acrophobia to be.

My acrophobia has actually got measurably worse with age, rather than better. I do genuinely feel that I am being drawn over the edge. Normally, of course, it's something that is easy to work around. I can plan not to set foot on cliff tops for example, or take steps to avoid fifteenth-floor balconies. Occasionally, however, real life creeps up on me and puts me, without warning, in situations which I'd prefer to avoid. A visit to the theatre is normally a pleasurable experience, but not if my ticket is for the front row of the balcony. I've been a quivering wreck, and suffered major embarrassment, in such diverse locations as the Kirov Theatre in St Petersburg and Trent Bridge cricket ground. It's strange in that I'm comfortable in aircraft and looking out of the windows of high-rise buildings, the key being that the phobia is inoperative if I am entirely contained and have no chance of falling, even if I wanted to. But if the location involved is open to the elements or does not provide absolutely foolproof, 100 per cent wraparound protection, then the onset of the shakes is not too far distant.

I walked through the centre of Inverness up to the bridge, past Inverness Caledonian Thistle's trim little football stadium and surveyed the lie of the land. There was a footpath on the bridge which, for ordinary folk, was absolutely fine. The whole set-up would have passed the most rigorous health and safety inspection. The railings were sturdy and quite high, and there was something of a gap between them and the footpath. It wasn't bad. In fact it was only a danger to folk who actually *wanted* to scale the fence and plunge hundreds of feet into the Firth below. The trouble was that that is precisely what my phobia impels me to try to do.

The fact that I considered a detour around the Beauly Firth, a distance of some 20 miles, is an indication of how seriously I was taking it all. But in the end, after a long pause, I decided that the configuration of railings and footpath was just about manageable. I covered the first yard, thinking there was only another 1,149 left to do. The sweat was pouring down my face.

I very soon discovered that I felt a lot better if I walked unnaturally close to the edge of the footpath, thereby maximizing the distance between me and the railing. The problem with this strategy was the fact that, at this stage of its development, the A9 is in full spate and much of the traffic is HGV. Every few seconds I was buffeted by the slipstream of some speeding behemoth and was in constant danger of being dragged to an alternative, and altogether more workaday death under the wheels of the northbound goods traffic.

Once on the bridge there was no turning back. I moved quickly and employed another ruse that had served me well in the past. I began to sing and shout. It was loud, it was tuneless and it was entirely random, but there was nobody there to hear it. The noise of my voice and of the traffic served as useful partial distractions.

On a couple of occasions the panic that was bubbling merrily below the surface almost broke through the thin crust of my resolve. If it had succeeded I would have been forced into my ultimate fall-back response. This had last been employed on a rocky hillside path in Petra (well I thought it was going to be OK, didn't I?) to my wife's almost terminal embarrassment. This was the *crawl*. I would have got down on my hands and knees, with my eyes 3 inches above the tarmac, and crawled my way to safety.

Cut to a transport cafe somewhere north of Inverness.

Lorry driver: 'Hey, Harry, guess what I've just seen on the bridge. An old bloke with a rucksack and his arse in the air *crawling* over to North Kessock. People choose some funny old ways of getting to John O'Groats these days.'

Thankfully this conversation never took place but it was a pretty close call.

It's difficult to describe how I felt as I came off the bridge. To say I felt l like I'd just cheated death is melodramatic but, in a sense, that's exactly what I *had* done. Perhaps a more rational comparison would be with the euphoria after an examination that has gone much better than expected, or how a politician feels after he's successfully come through an interview with Jeremy Paxman.

I let my legs recover their strength, took a few photographs of the bridge and pottered around the lovely village of North Kessock in the morning sunshine. I passed a targe manufacturer, which is not something you do every day. A targe is one of those round Highland battle shields, made of wood and covered in leather, often with a circular boss or spike in the centre. In North Kessock this was, quite literally, a cottage industry.

I was far too preoccupied to take it in, but before going on to the bridge I'd passed a sign informing me that John O'Groats was still 120 miles distant. It was time to return to business.

The morning's walk took me over the Black Isle, which is not an isle at all but a peninsula bounded by the Moray and Cromarty Firths. It's a pleasantly low-rise, wooded, agricultural area and I made good time on country lanes up through Munlochy, past the signpost to the Black Isle Brewery and onward to Culbokie. I filled in the time by booking my accommodation for the next two nights. It seemed to me that every prospective B&B landlady I spoke to was Janet, the housekeeper in *Dr Finlay's Casebook*. The voices seemed uncannily similar. There was one possible exception where I believe I might have had a brief but pleasant conversation, not with Janet, but with her mother. I looked forward to seeing whether the reality corresponded to my imagination.

I lunched on a bench in the village of Culbokie with a panoramic view of Cromarty Firth. I was much taken with a placard for the local newspaper. It was the *Press and Journal*, the self-styled 'Voice of the North', and today's big news was 'Highlands Divided in Parking Charge Row'. If, after centuries of internecine strife, parking charges were the only remaining issue that divided the clans, then we really were in severe danger of making some progress.

Truth to tell, however, my mind wasn't really on parking charges. I was contemplating another bridge. After the terrors of Kessock I was now confronted with another road bridge over a firth and I had a good view of it from my lunch venue.

It didn't actually look that bad. Long, certainly, but this one wasn't a suspension bridge – it was supported on stilts at what appeared to be a manageable height over the waters of Cromarty Firth. And when I got down there I found I was right. It would, in fact, have been easier to fall off this bridge than off its counterpart at Kessock. And there's absolutely no doubt that if I *had* fallen off, death would have been a 100 per cent cast-iron certainty. But the point at issue was this: the fall wouldn't have killed me. I'd have drowned as sure as eggs are eggs, but the bridge just wasn't high enough to bring the dreaded phobia into play.

The bridge had taken the A9 over the Firth but I soon escaped off the main highway and took a minor road to Evanton. It was here that I visited what must be a contender for the title of the world's smallest library. I called in with a view to updating the blog and, at a stroke, halved the amount of available remaining space after allowing for the librarian and her modest desk in the corner of the room. My rucksack also absorbed a few precious square feet of floor space, so when I vacated the computer terminal and said my farewells I think the librarian was genuinely thankful. While I'd been treated in a civil and helpful fashion, I hadn't been on the receiving end of the jocular small talk and smiling encouragement that had been meted out to me by other librarians all the way since Okehampton. I think she was just relieved to see her library freed up again for use by less malodorous users.

Alness is a little one-street town which has been both a 'Scotland in Bloom' and 'Britain in Bloom' winner. There were hanging baskets everywhere and I liked it. I also liked Rina and her excellent B&B, which abutted directly on to the Inverness–Thurso railway line.

It had been a long and eventful day – 21 miles to Alness. I'd now done 994 miles altogether. Tomorrow morning I'd do the thousandth. I was getting close now – only six days to go and I was beginning to detect the onset of mild paranoia about the prospect of injury or illness. It would, to say the very least, be galling to have to drop out at this late stage, particularly as I'd withstood everything the West Highland Way and the Kessock Bridge could throw at me. It only needed one split second's carelessness or one fleeting moment of inattention. 'Blease? Oh yeah, he was the guy who was 20 miles short of John O'Groats and then fell over. Had to give up. Clown.'

Wednesday 28 June was another sunny day. I felt that my choice of route that morning was validated by the fact that it was National Cycle Route 1. It hadn't been marked on my map as such, but I was clearly developing the same unerring eye for a route as the deities who ordain the cycle-track network. I'd actually begun the day with a bizarre and slightly alarming experience. On climbing out of my comfortable bed at Rina's I'd immediately turned on the TV. Standing in front of it, yawning and scratching, I was startled to be suddenly confronted, at a range of some 18 inches, by the face of an old university friend that I hadn't seen in 30 years. I'd missed the start of the item, but having recovered from my initial shock, I was able to catch its general drift. My old mate seemed to be talking about the side effects of certain drugs used to counter high blood pressure and (Good God!) the associated problems of impotence. He looked grey and ill and depressed – and it made me think for about the three millionth time how lucky I was to be doing what I was doing.

It was a pleasant, straight, country lane between Alness and Tain, Scotland's Oldest Royal Burgh, which sits on the southern edge of the Dornoch Firth. I walked through gentle rolling terrain with occasional glimpses of Cromarty Firth over to the right. On the surface of the Firth sat a gigantic parked oil rig. I was in Tain by lunchtime and ate my sandwich in a small park in the town centre. Here was another place where it would have been good to linger. There was an exhibition with the nice alliterative title of 'Tain through Time'. I passed the striking memorial to the 8,400 men of the Seaforth Highlanders who gave their lives in the Great War and then a splendid building that formerly housed the Tain Royal Academy. It was opened in 1813 and, according to a helpful information board, among the subjects taught were 'The Elements of Fortification and Gunnery'.

Tain is also the home of the Glenmorangie Distillery, which I passed on my way down to the bridge across the Dornoch Firth. Thankfully, the bridge proved to be a re-run of its Cromarty counterpart rather than the monster at Kessock and at its end I entered the County of Sutherland. And then another pleasant minor road into Dornoch itself. Since leaving Inverness my only contact with the A9 had been on the three major bridges. As I got further north I knew that the alternatives would narrow and that the A9 would figure more prominently.

The key event of the day was the call from Roy and Maureen to tell me that they'd breasted the tape at John O'Groats. Which was gratifying. But not nearly as gratifying as the news that, amazingly, they also planned to be in Dornoch that evening. What a brilliant story-book coincidence! I somehow couldn't imagine it being a sober, low-key reunion.

The Royal Burgh of Dornoch has a cathedral and, reminiscent of Truro and Lichfield, my B&B was right next door. While I waited for Roy and Maureen I had a look around Dornoch. I'd never been to this part of the world before and expected a dour and rugged kind of place. My pre-conception was miles out. Dornoch is a handsome and elegant place. The cathedral appears deceptively squat and cramped from the outside but the interior is spacious, plain, dignified and impressive. The stained-glass windows were beautiful in the early evening sunlight.

I duly convened at the Dornoch Inn with Roy and Maureen, accompanied by their son-in-law, Ian. They had turned the last stage of the walk into a family holiday and had used Dornoch as a base while Ian backed them up in the car and ferried them 'home' after each day's walking. I admired Ian. He was exposed to massive doses of route boredom that would have floored anyone with an average constitution, but he stayed bravely on his feet despite several rounds of exceptionally heavy punishment. I suppose that with Roy and Maureen as in-laws his immune system would, over time, have developed a high degree of natural resistance.

It was great to see them again. We'd all gone through a lot since saying farewell on the road out of Launceston, and it was the first time that I'd been able to share my thoughts with anyone who'd ground their way through the same whole end-to-end process. They were naturally delighted at what they'd achieved and both looked incredibly fit. I expressed mild surprise, given the difference in our speeds during the Cornish leg of the walk, that they were only five days in front of me. The answer lay in the different routes we'd taken. Roy and Maureen had taken a route through the Pennines and a consequently longer itinerary through Southern Scotland. Roy estimated their total mileage at 1,200 – around 100 more than my own projected final total. I let them into the hallowed secret of the Bollin Valley Way and the access it gave to the canals in Lancashire. I told them about my cunning plan for Southern Scotland and my successful crossing of the Glasgow conurbation. Roy listened to all this route talk very carefully and then nodded his approval. I was a happy man.

The next day, Thursday 29 June, was going to be another memorable one. Perhaps understandably, I didn't feel too sharp in the initial phases of the day, but the bracing walk out of Dornoch northwards over its golf links cleared my head beautifully. This was just as well because it was going to be another day of reunion. As I progressed up the coast towards Embo (twinned, unbelievably, with Kaunakakai in Hawaii), my wife was attempting one of the most ambitious

217

and intricate journeys it is possible to make in mainland Britain. Her journey from rural Norfolk to a rendezvous with me in Brora was involving a complex and volatile combination of air, rail and road transport. It had taken days of planning and, privately, despite what it said on the timetables, I didn't rate her chances of arriving the same day as more than 50/50.

In fact reunions were coming thick and fast. First Roy and Maureen, now Jane, and then Neil was planning to join us for the weekend. It was like the end of a Christmas pantomime where all the characters, even the ones who've died, come together on stage for the rousing finale. I thought I'd better contact Peter in case he was available. And Dave Dobson might fancy a pub crawl round John O'Groats.

Embo had some award-winning beaches but it wasn't exactly Waikiki. I pressed on to Loch Fleet, which gives directly on to the sea, thereby impeding the walker's progress up the coast and forcing me inland on to the A9. There was plenty of bird life and a few basking seals as I walked around the shore of the loch.

It wasn't enjoyable walking on the A9, but at this juncture (and with increasing frequency from here on) there was no alternative. The walk along the A9 to Golspie took me around 90 minutes. Back in Carlisle, Dave, the north–south end-to-ender, had warned me that it was an unpleasant road, and he wasn't wrong. It was busy and fast and there wasn't always a verge. On the plus side, it was usually quite straight so that motorists and pedestrians could see each other coming from a long way off. I had lunch sitting on the beach at Golspie, the first time I'd done this since day two of the walk on the South West Coast Path between Penzance and Helston. And it was then a pleasant 5-mile walk along the coastal path past Dunrobin Castle, the ancestral home of the Earls of Sutherland, to Brora.

I'd been keeping track of Jane's fluctuating fortunes,

mobile phone reception permitting, throughout the day and, much to my surprise, it now looked as if she was going to beat me to it. It would have improved the whole story if Jane, having arrived in Brora, had walked down the beach to meet me. A gradual, carefully choreographed convergence against a vast background of sea and sky, with appropriate backing music of course, would have been a romantic masterpiece, a potential milestone in cinema history. Instead, we settled for a more prosaic reunion in the forecourt of our B&B.

Given the need to maintain high standards during Jane's stints on the trail, I'd chosen our accommodation in Brora with care and it didn't disappoint. Our host was Alistair, whose worthy establishment had, he informed us, once played host to the US ambassador. The man had also been engaged on an end-to-end walk, albeit one undertaken in phases. Not only had Alistair had to contend with the ambassador, but he'd also accommodated his extensive retinue of bodyguards and assistants.

Jane and I walked north the next morning over Brora's golf links and then, for a short spell along the beach. We trespassed very briefly on the railway line before eventually being forced on to the A9. We hadn't been too concerned about traffic on the railway as there are only three trains a day in each direction. I reflected, however, that a century ago this single-line track between Inverness and Thurso would have been one of the most strategic pieces of railway line in the British Empire. It provided all-important, land-based communication with Scapa Flow in the Orkneys, home of the Grand Fleet, the great, grey iron fortresses that made Britain *the* superpower of the time.

Once we were on the A9 we were on it virtually the whole of the rest of the way to Helmsdale. We were able to make a brief detour off the main road for lunch but, even then, the venue only satisfied about 27 per cent of the requirements set down by Jane for a lunch location. We passed the plaque marking the spot 'near which the last wolf in Sutherland was killed by the hunter Polson in or about the year 1700'. It's a most unremarkable memorial but, for some strange reason, it gets a mention, often a photograph, in just about every piece of end-to-end literature that's ever been published. There's even a picture of it in Brian Smailes' book alongside Brian's more normal diet of roundabouts, road signs and dual carriageways. I think the reason for its popularity is that it provides a fleeting moment of levity and interest in the otherwise unremitting tedium of the A9.

Helmsdale is a splendid little place. Jane and I arrived in mid-afternoon, went to the library to update the blog and had a wander around the harbour. We then visited the Mirage Café, a renowned local restaurant, and according to (if my memory serves me correctly) Clarissa Dickson-Wright, one of the UK's top ten fish-and-chip restaurants. Photographs on the wall showed a lady bearing an uncanny resemblance to Barbara Cartland, presumably the owner, greeting a number of distinguished clients, ranging eclectically from that distinguished end-to-ender Sir Ian Botham through David Seaman to the (presumably less athletic) Countess of Raine. Like other fish-and-chip establishments I'd come across in Scotland, the Mirage had a number of additional strings to its bow. It was afternoon tea time so Jane and I went for a magnificent strawberry meringue concoction that was another speciality of the house. It was absolutely heaped with whipped cream and was already giving me the sugar rush of a lifetime. But the waitress, God bless her, was worried that we weren't getting enough. She brought a jug of pouring cream to put the finishing touch to this monster confection and was surprised and alarmed when we declined. Here was another place that was laudably maintaining the high standards set down by the Scottish Cholesterol Marketing Board.

Helmsdale was radically expanded in the early 1800s to

accommodate victims of the Highland clearances. Some stayed to try and make a living out of fishing, but others emigrated to seek a new life in Australia, New Zealand, the USA and elsewhere. A large memorial statue commemorating the emigrants overlooks the town. It's a moving and effective piece of statuary. It made an excellent destination for an evening stroll as we attempted to work the Mirage Café's sugar out of our systems.

Jane and I left the Bridge Hotel early the next morning, Saturday 1 July. I'd worked out the latest in a series of cunning plans that would enable us to cover the 15 miles to Dunbeath and still see England's World Cup quarter-final game in comfort that afternoon. Execution of the cunning plan would have been impossible without Neil. Having been of immense logistical assistance at the start of the West Highland Way, Neil was now insisting on making the 600-mile round trip from Lochwinnoch to give further impetus to the campaign.

There was to be no escape from the A9 that day but at least the weather was fine and we had superb coastal scenery. We entered Caithness, the final county of the walk. I'd estimated that Neil would be with us by 10 a.m. and it was, in fact, 9.53 when his car drew up alongside us. He'd driven 290 miles that morning. I didn't have the nerve to ask about his average speed. Instead, I rather ungratefully queried his sanity in driving so far to spend two days walking up the A9. On the contrary, he replied, people in Lochwinnoch (he meant, presumably, the drinkers in The Brown Bull) thought it was a wonderful idea and were agog with excitement to see how it all turned out. Neil then drove on to Dunbeath, relieving us of our rucksacks in the process. The next step of the cunning plan would have him walking back to meet us and then accompanying us back to Dunbeath and the car.

The plan unfolded as intended – even down to the pork pies for lunch. We met Neil striding down the road to meet us

221

as we climbed out of Berriedale and reached the village of Dunbeath at 2 p.m. We were 40 miles from John O'Groats.

The cunning plan now entered one of its more complex phases. Having made it to Dunbeath we now retreated in the car back to Helmsdale. I'd identified the residents' lounge of the Bridge Hotel as a very comfortable place to watch the football, and now free of the dead weight of peer pressure and relieved of the expectations of friends and family, Neil felt able to relax and watch as well.

It was fitting in a way that, having lived with England's World Cup quest since Land's End, I should now see it grind to an ignominious halt as my own odyssey was drawing to a close. Exultant at the recuperation of his metatarsal, Wayne drove it unerringly into the unprotected groin of an opponent and his resultant red card virtually ended England's hopes of further progress. It was ironic that, in adversity, the team produced what was probably its most robust performance of the tournament, but it was still a major disappointment to lose to a mediocre Portuguese side.

It was noticeable that Scolari, the Portuguese manager, had managed to extract far more from his own exceptionally average collection of players than Sven Goran Eriksson had from what, on paper at least, was an infinitely more talented group of individuals. It was final confirmation, if one were needed, of Eriksson's status as an out-and-out charlatan. The lack of success in major competitions, the ridiculous salary, the stupid haircut – they were all major vexations, but what galled me most about Eriksson was his total apparent inability to grasp the importance of his role and the major responsibility it entailed. The £5m salary might have given him a clue, but he still had the effrontery to complain of media intrusiveness in the apparent belief that he could earn that amount of money, knowingly occupy a role that carried the hopes and expectations of millions, but *still* be immune from scrutiny when two-timing his partner or illicitly pursuing alternative job opportunities. The manager of the Swedish team had confided to the media that he drew a salary equating to 1 per cent of Eriksson's, and labelled the remuneration package of his compatriot as 'obscene'. That Saturday afternoon in Helmsdale it was hard to disagree.

Never mind – the atmosphere over there in Gelsenkirchen might have been gloomy but here in Helmsdale it was 'Hoolie' night. I had to confess to complete ignorance as to the meaning of the word. The dictionary definition of a 'hoolie' is a high wind, but in the context of Helmsdale on 1 July the meaning is more akin to Gala Day à la Lockerbie but without any attendant need for tiresome and wasteful preliminaries like pipe bands or processions. The basic idea appeared to be to get straight down to the serious business of revelry. Neil, Jane and I took a stroll around town after dinner but saw very little evidence of revelry, which was rather a shame. Jane professed to have been awoken by returning revellers at some ungodly hour of the morning but that, unfortunately, was the sum total of our involvement. I was ashamed of myself. In our younger days Neil and I would have gone and looked for the hoolie – we wouldn't have sat back and waited for the hoolie to find us.

Sunday 2 July, and in theory the penultimate day of the walk. The next phase of the cunning plan saw Neil driving us back to Dunbeath, dropping us there minus our rucksacks and then driving on. He left the car at Camster and walked back to meet us. We'd enjoyed the Caithness coastline but today it was flatter, bleaker and less interesting. It wasn't set off to best advantage by the heavily overcast conditions. Taken overall, it was probably one of the least inspiring day's walking of the entire trip. Just after Lybster we left the main road and turned due north up a dead straight road through an increasingly flat, bleak and barren landscape. It was a relief to be clear of the traffic, but after a short while the dwellings ended and there was nothing but wild moorland and the occasional plantation of conifers.

Neil had parked his car at the Grey Cairns of Camster, two large Neolithic chambered cairns dating from the Stone Age around 5,000 years ago. They'd been restored and it was possible to crawl through the narrow entrance along a short tunnel into the central chamber. Perhaps predictably, Neil and I played infantile games, taking photographs of each other's backsides disappearing into the cairn, before Neil decided it was time to go and embarked upon the 300-mile drive back to Lochwinnoch. For the second time on the walk he'd provided invaluable assistance at a crucial time, as well as being excellent company.

Jane and I carried on to Watten, a small settlement on the main Wick–Thurso road, now, of course, carrying our rucksacks. It was hard going, with nothing to relieve the monotony. We covered 21 miles that day, with the prospect for the morrow of another 18 to John O'Groats across similar terrain. There was going to be no easy finish to the walk.

That evening Jane and I embarked on the first of a series of lasts. Cathy's spacious B&B would be the final B&B of the trip and the Brown Trout at Watten the last pub at which we'd seek refreshment. The Brown Trout was a homely little pub but the meagre selection of beers precluded further work on the research project.

On the final morning there was an echo of the feeling of unreality that I'd experienced that first morning at Land's End. Whereas at Land's End the prospect of a 1,100-mile walk had seemed utterly outlandish, now it was difficult to conceive of stopping. This was what I *did* wasn't it? I walked. What other kind of life was there?

That last morning's walk was rugged and bleak. It had rained overnight and the weather was overcast and miserable. Jane found the going hard and, like the previous afternoon, there was precious little in the landscape to divert her mind from the pain in her toes. Over to the east across the moorland we could make out Noss Head and its lighthouse, but then that too disappeared in the gloom.

We went through the hamlet of Lyth and were then confronted with an apparently endless, dead straight road which gently undulated its way to the horizon. Despite our best efforts we only seemed to be making a negligible impression on it, and Jane's toes were getting worse. There wasn't the remotest prospect of finding a lunch venue that came anywhere close to satisfying Jane's criteria. There wasn't even a wall we could sit on. So eventually we gave up and sat on the edge of the road with our feet in the ditch. Sad, in a way, that our last lunch location should be so rudimentary. On we went. The only slight potential consolation was a small, indefinable difference in the quality of the light ahead, that might, just might, betoken a transition from land to sea.

Then, after hours of monotony and gloom, within moments, our fortunes were transformed. We crested the latest in a series of undulations but there, this time, rather than moorland, was the sea and even, would you believe it, an Orkney or two. I'd never seen one before. And almost at that precise moment, as if the whole thing had been stage-managed by a director of exceptionally melodramatic bent, the sun came out and bathed everything in a beautiful, cool, fresh light. Both sea and sky were a pale, washed blue. John O'Groats was out of sight to the north-east over on our right but we could see for miles along the coast to the west and ahead to the islands. Cue a thousand violins. It was breathtaking.

Suddenly there were habitations again. We walked through Upper Gills and then cut eastwards down into the village of Canisbay, enjoying all the while the view over to Stroma, the nearest Orkney, and to other more distant islands. I'd been much taken with some of the war memorials I'd seen in the far north of Scotland and the one in Canisbay, with the ringing prose of its inscription, was particularly fine. On a lighter note was a house with the enigmatic name of 'Aargh' and if the name board had been in a more accessible place I might have stood beside it for a commemorative photograph. What did it mean? Was it Gaelic? Or was it the creation of a resident of English extraction with a peculiar sense of humour? I'd dearly love to know.

Quite soon we were standing at the end of the short stretch of road that leads down from the actual village of John O'Groats to the small collection of shops and stalls that represent the ceremonial heart of the place. The last quarter mile. It was a moment to savour. Monday 3 July 2006. 4 p.m. We stood and savoured, but there's a limit to the amount of savouring you can do. So we set off down the hill into the car park, went round to the pub at the back and crossed the finishing line.

13

I made it to Lords. And our daughter's wedding passed off wonderfully well. The return to real life was actually very pleasurable in many respects. Just ordinary things like home cooking and clean clothes. And of course it was great to see family and friends again. Everyone was very complimentary – Phil the vicar even led a round of applause in church. I also took advantage of my enhanced fitness levels to do the Great North Run, a half marathon, run in Newcastle by about 50,000 other crazy people.

I totted up the statistics of the walk. 76 days. 1,096 miles. 41 Ordnance Survey maps. 2 pairs of boots. I also totted up the money I'd raised and was amazed at people's generosity. In many respects the walk had been a supreme piece of self indulgence, but the fundraising served to partially salve my conscience. I felt that the £13,000 I'd received by way of pledges or donations was a sum that might help my chosen causes actually get a few things done.

Predictably the walk soon started to acquire a rosy hue, possibly even the beginnings of a halo. Certain parts of it began to appear more enjoyable in retrospect than they were at the time. It's possible to laugh now about the Kessock Bridge and the mud in Staffordshire and it's only right and natural that perspectives should change in this way.

One part of the walk that will, of course, always retain something of a sheen is the afternoon of our arrival. Jane and

I pottered around in the sunshine, had an ice cream and a cup of tea and went to the little museum. No whoops of joy, no pumping of fists in the air, it just felt rather pleasant and ordinary. I was delighted that Jane was there to share the moment.

It was essential that, having 'checked in' by signing the book at Lands End, I should now 'check out' by signing its counterpart at John O'Groats. Bizarrely, there are two, one in the souvenir shop and one in the pub, so for the avoidance of all doubt I signed them both. I was looking for the entry by Roy and Maureen and found it in the book at the pub (of course). After the details of their arrival date and time, and the obligatory two lines of comment, they'd written 'Hope you get to read this, Steve'. Just for a second it was lump-in-throat time.

We went to have our photographs taken by the side of the ceremonial signpost and were amused to meet a couple of bikers who'd just completed the journey from Land's End in 18 hours. They thought 76 days was ridiculously slow. Because we'd spent so much time fiddling around after our arrival the bloke who takes the photographs had closed down for the day, so we had to put all our walking gear and rucksacks on the next morning and line up by the signpost again. I didn't feel that well – just possibly as a result of the celebration we'd had at the hotel the previous evening with two groups of jubilant end-to-end cyclists. But it was worth it for the photograph. It brings a smile every time I see it.

And that was it. Final impressions? Well, I'm pleased I did it. I've no particular sense of pride. I just trudged unspectacularly for a few weeks, and all the walk did was provide further evidence that plodding persistence will usually be rewarded. I enjoyed seeing the UK in a way that I'd never seen it before and the beer tasting was good too. I even got to find out a little about Scottish beers, a subject which hitherto had been a closed book.

Has the walk changed me? I don't believe so. The strange flashes of patience and growing inclination to behave philosophically soon disappeared when I returned to the real world. No, I guess the main residual impressions are twofold. Firstly how wonderfully liberating and increasingly addictive it was to live the life of a quasi-vagrant. The pleasure and anticipation of pushing off each morning stayed with me right to the end. Secondly, and perhaps most importantly, I was struck by the unfailing kindness and helpfulness of people throughout the entire journey. There was barely a cross word or mean-spirited action throughout the whole 1,096 miles. We read and hear so much about the baser side of human nature that it was reassuring to see an almost infinite variety of people, mainly, of course, complete strangers, responding and behaving with such unerring generosity, courtesy and humour.

Would I recommend it? Certainly! If you're motivated, then go for it. I suppose if you analyse it, there are three main obstacles – fitness, money and time. If you're reasonably able-bodied, fitness is something you can work on. It's unwise to step off the train at Penzance without being reasonably confident that you can cover, say, 10–12 miles in a day and then, importantly, repeat the performance without too much difficulty the following day, and then again the day after that. If you're not already match fit then the training will take a little time and persistence but it shouldn't prove insuperable.

Money is clearly an issue. I abandoned any pretence at financial control for the periods when Jane was with me but I kept track of daily expenses quite rigorously for the time I was alone. The average total daily outgo was around £47 which means a total spend for the walk of around £3,500. That's an awful lot of money. But do bear in mind it includes the cost of things like toothpaste and newspapers which you'd be spending money on whatever you were doing. And the same, of course, applies to food. Moreover, while I wasn't extravagant, it would certainly be possible to do an end-to-end walk more cheaply by making use of campsites and youth hostels and, if you have the patience or stamina, by cooking your own food. It's also not compulsory to spend vast sums on beer. And when you come to think of it, £3,500 isn't bad value for money for a 'holiday' that lasts 10 weeks or more. In everything that I've read about the Lands End–John O'Groats walk, and in all my conversations on the subject, I've never heard the subject of money put forward as a serious barrier. If you want it badly enough you'll find a way.

Time, however, is clearly a potential show-stopper. It's obviously possible to complete the walk significantly faster than my exceptionally pedestrian time of 76 days. But even so, unless you are in the fortunate position, as I was, of having a longer than normal period of work-free time available, then the sheer length of the walk will be a problem. Which is, I suppose, why most people, rather than proceed on foot, cover the distance by cycle (or, if you can only spare 24 hours, like my biker friends, on a Harley Davidson). One common solution to the problem is to do the walk in instalments, using successive holidays to cover the trail in manageable chunks.

So why not give it a go? Drop in on Pippa and enjoy the beautiful village of Belstone. Go to Arnside and watch the sun set over the Kent Estuary. Try the Queen's Arms in Bosley and ask Janet to make you a cheese sandwich. Find out how it feels to walk underneath an airport. All kinds of things will happen to you on the way. You might fall over. You might not like the beer. You might, on the other hand, meet all kinds of good people and have a supremely convivial time. The walk might change you – and there again it might not. It might be the spiritual uplift of a lifetime or a terrible pain-wracked odyssey.

But whatever it turns out to be, it's something you'll remember for the rest of your life.